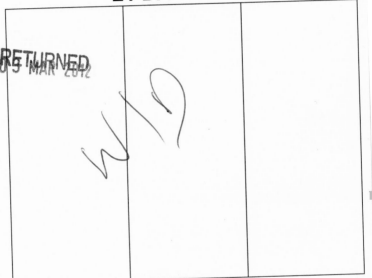

Skills

Roy Bailey

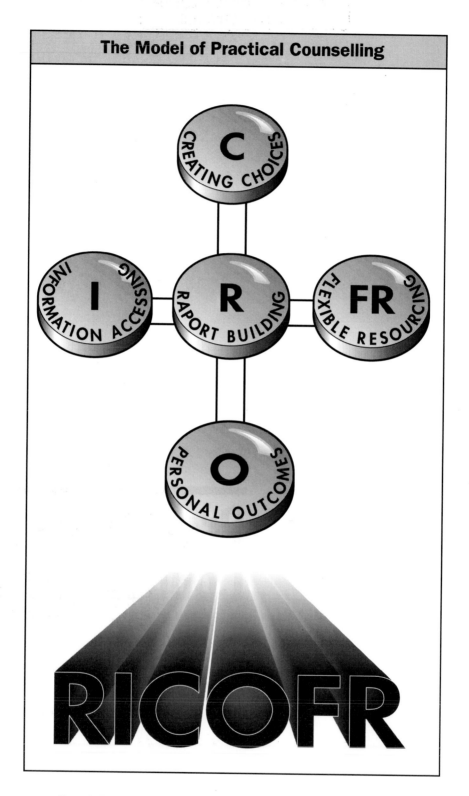

The Model of Practical Counselling

C — CREATING CHOICES
I — INFORMATION ACCESSING
R — RAPORT BUILDING
FR — FLEXIBLE RESOURCING
O — PERSONAL OUTCOMES

RICOFR

See *A Practical Model for Practical Counselling*, page 66

HELPING PEOPLE CHANGE:
THE ESSENTIAL
COUNSELLING SERIES

Practical Counselling Skills

Roy Bailey

WINSLOW

Telford Road • Bicester
Oxon OX6 0TS • UK

DEDICATION
To Felicity and Fraser

First published in 1993 by
Winslow Press Limited, Telford Road, Bicester, Oxon OX6 0TS
Reprinted 1994, 1995
© Roy Bailey, 1993

Typeset by Gecko Limited, Bicester, Oxon

02-1542 Printed in Great Britain by Quorn Litho, Loughborough

British Library Cataloguing in Publication Data
Bailey, Roy
    Practical Counselling Skills – (Helping People Change: the Essential
    Counselling Series)
    I. Title   II. Series
    361.3

ISBN 0–86388–116-5

CONTENTS

Dr Roy Bailey PhD MA DACP MITD AFBPsS DipEH P NLP CPsychol is a chartered clinical psychologist, counsellor, psychotherapist, trainer and qualified hypnotherapist. He is Principal of the Centre for Counselling and Integrative Therapy which provides client services and staff training in practical counselling, cognitive psychotherapy neuro-linguistic programming and hypnotherapy. Roy is also a director of Peak Performance Management Ltd and a founding partner of the Personal Power Institute, a teaching institute based in London concerned with increasing motivation and extending the personal potential of children and adults.

His other books and publications include *Coping with Stress in Caring, Stress and Coping in Nursing, Systematic Relaxation, 50 Activities for Managing Stress* and *50 Activities for Developing Counselling Skills*.

PREFACE TO THE SERIES

Welcome to *Helping People Change: the Essential Counselling Series*. Counselling skills are now becoming more and more recognized as an essential part of effective helping. Nowhere is this more true than in social services, education, the health care professions and their associates. In publishing this series Winslow has produced a range of books on different approaches to counselling that should be of immediate practical benefit to anyone in the 'people business'. Each book in the series is written by experienced counsellors respected in their own field. Each title reveals a different way in which you can develop your counselling skills with your clients. I hope you will find them a welcome and close companion in your work.

ROY BAILEY
Series Editor

ACKNOWLEDGEMENTS

Many people make this book possible. In different ways they have all played an important part in my life, and in the writing of this book.

In particular I would very much like to thank: Carl Rogers for sowing the seeds in my thinking that formed the foundation for the development of practical counselling; Will Schutz for his stimulating and inspirational insights about the fundamental personal needs of people; Milton Erickson for showing me how nothing need ever be wasted in counselling sessions with clients; William Glasser for his revelations about personal responsibility in counselling and therapy.

I would equally like to thank: my partners at The Centre for Counselling and Integrative Therapy, and Peak Performance Management Ltd for their useful discussions about counselling people and counselling in organizations; fellow clinical psychologists, colleagues, students in healthcare, social services and education for their growing interest in practical counselling; the editorial team at Winslow for their encouragement and support to write this, the first book in the new *Helping People Change: the Essential Counselling Series*.

Finally, I should acknowledge all of my clients who have taught me about human courage and the dignity of living.

INTRODUCTION

Counselling has arrived in health care. An understanding of what counselling is and how it is practised is essential for anyone who purports to practise counselling, but too much time has been wasted talking about definitions of counselling. In fact many of the discussions, workshops and courses on counselling have actually held back the advance of counselling in health care and those who provide it. I do not intend to extend this debate. This book is about the practical counselling skills I use in my work with clients. It is a book about helping, and how practical counselling skills can be used to empower other people to help themselves.

The views on practical counselling skills I express may not necessarily be those which other counsellors agree with. That is no bad thing because counselling is always a live, changing and dynamic experience both for those who practise counselling skills and for the clients who participate in the counselling process.

Who This Book is For

This book is for anyone in the health and caring professions who uses counselling skills in their daily contact with clients. Equally, essential counselling should be of interest to those who want to begin to use counselling skills in their work with others. This book is also for those in the health and allied care professions who want to use essential counselling skills as 'a stepping stone' to further study and practice of counselling. This book is for all of these people. In this sense, essential counselling skills should prove to be of great value and benefit to nurses, doctors, speech therapists, occupational therapists, radiographers, physiotherapists, social workers, teachers and many others. But most of all this book is for the clients who are receivers of caring. If essential counselling skills have anything to offer them it will be a greater sensitivity and effectiveness in the quality of care they receive from the caring professions. Essential counselling, I believe, goes some way to providing the understanding and necessary skills that can improve the quality of client care.

What is in This Book

•

This book, the first in the *Helping People Change: the Essential Counselling Series*, introduces you to the wide range of fundamental knowledge and skills you need to begin counselling. The knowledge and skills you can develop are based on a clear and practical model of counselling. In addition to this I have included many cases where counselling skills were essential to helping clients. In these cases you will learn how the counsellor worked with the client and see the relevance of using specific counselling skills with particular problems. Knowing what is in this book is like being able to read a map. First get to know the shape of the map and the territory it covers. Once you have done that and you know your way about the map you can then begin to make some journeys into counselling. As you continue to make new discoveries about the contents of the book you can plan even more ambitious adventures into counselling. The counselling skills in this book are like signposts that make up the map of counselling. The clearer your signposts and the more relevant your map, the more you will be able to understand and use the skills of essential counselling.

How to Use this Book

•

Using this book is a bit like taking a journey in Aladdin's cave. You know there are some precious gems of counselling to be discovered. You remember that Aladdin had a genie in a magic lamp that produced wondrous results. The counselling concepts, counselling skills and cases in this book are just like that. They can help you to help others achieve their goals and overcome their problems. But like Aladdin you need to work at polishing the lamp. Polishing your counselling skills can be done in at least five ways.

First, you can practise the skills and understanding of counselling with your clients and colleagues. Second, you can become adept at relating what you do with your clients to the concepts and models of counselling. Third, you can learn from the cases how counselling skills can be cultivated to a high degree of sophistication. Fourth, you can use the different parts of this book as if you were using a shopping list in a supermarket. You can select and choose the kinds of concepts, skills and model of counselling you need, at the time, which are most likely to produce the best 'menu' to help your clients. You can freely photocopy the assignments and exercises for this purpose. Fifth, you can further expand your knowledge and level of competence in counselling skills by going on an appropriate counselling course.

Although there are different ways of using this book they all have a single purpose: to open up new options in helping your clients to create choices about the way they live their lives.

Note: Many of the case examples in this book are derived from practical counselling sessions. The real identities of these cases have been removed and examples changed in the interests of protecting the clients.

Chapter 1

THE PURPOSES OF PRACTICAL COUNSELLING

Influencing Clients

•

Practical counselling is very clear in what it sets out to achieve. First of all it sets out to influence events. A close consideration of counselling literature and of practising counsellors shows that counselling, when it is effective and practical, is about influencing. When you are practising counselling skills you are, wittingly or unwittingly, influencing your client. The vast body of knowledge about communication between people has a valid message for all who are engaged in practical counselling. You are influencing whether you like it or not. So be aware of the influencing effects you have on others when you are engaged in practical counselling.

This influence can have several strands to it. If you are offering practical counselling to someone, you may want to influence the situation they find themselves in. Or you may want to influence the perceptions or views they have about themselves or their circumstances. Another purpose of practical counselling may be to enable clients or patients to review their specific concerns and decide that they do not want change in their lives or their situation at present. Yet another purpose of practical counselling is to help people discover resources in themselves they never thought they possessed that will give them the motivation and the will to change themselves or their situation.

Rallying Rapport

•

One of the main tasks for the counsellor, and a central purpose of practical counselling, is building rapport. Why? Because without it there can be no influencing, and without that effective counselling cannot take place. The aim of providing practical counselling that will genuinely help people to identify, face up to, and overcome their personal problems simply fails when an affinity has not been established between the carer offering counselling and those expecting help. Counselling without establishing rapport is like expecting a fish to swim without water. Accord should be achieved at the outset of your contact with clients and carried on throughout your counselling contact with them. Don't start from the time your client walks into your clinic, consulting room or counselling session, but sooner. A bond can be established at the time of first talking to the client on the phone. The first time you send out an appointment to a client start building rapport. Use the first, and every other, occasion when you notice each other in the waiting room as an opportunity to build and strengthen your relationship. These are all occasions when opportunities for rapport are abundant. So if you want to achieve the purposes of practical counselling, give yourself this task and pursue it vigilantly. Establish rapport with your clients as soon as you can.

It is also critical that you maintain your rapport throughout practical counselling. If your understanding breaks down at any point during your counselling sessions you run a great risk of prematurely ending them, because rapport is so essential for influencing and change. Many a promising counselling session has evaporated and ended in frustration for counsellors and their clients when their bond has been irretrievably broken. But there is also good news. When you get into difficulties with counselling, rallying and recovering rapport can strengthen the bases from which further counselling activity can take place. Rallying rapport provides us with the opportunity to work intimately with clients who come for counselling. Breaking it loses that intimacy and inhibits the search for solutions and any action which clients might take to change themselves or their future. Appropriate attention to creating and maintaining rapport is necessary if you want to make practical progress in counselling clients.

Getting Information

●

Having rapport also allows us to search for information that is relevant and important to the client. In my experience, sometimes counsellors are so enthusiastic about getting information to help clients that they forget to first build enough rapport between themselves and their clients. This often results in the fruitless exchange of questions by the counsellor and lack of interest and uninvolved answers from clients. The fruit comes later. First rally and establish rapport and then you increase the probability of discovering information that has meaning for the client. Taking this approach may be difficult, but no one ever said counselling was easy.

Why should we make these checks and take these precautions to ensure we establish rapport with our clients and then seek information? It is simple. Information empowers clients. It does this in a number of ways. First of all many clients who come to counselling are confused and low in self-esteem. They lack confidence. They see themselves as having problems and having failed to resolve these problems. They blame themselves. They blame their friends, their spouses, their children. They blame their counsellors. Other clients come saying they know exactly what their problems are and how they can solve them. Yet they still have personal difficulties and they expect the counsellor to solve their problems for them or with them. So what do you do in situations like this? The novice carer providing practical counselling might be tempted to 'rush in where angels fear to tread' and provide a 'solution' for the client. But what is needed early in counselling sessions is information. Indeed relevant information is required throughout the process of practical counselling. The client needs information and so does the counsellor. When you practise counselling you should learn to employ the skills that will obtain the necessary information that both clients and counsellors need.

Imagine yourself in a library for a moment. There are millions of pieces of information in the library and you cannot possibly attend to all of them. So you select the information you want to study, explore, examine, question, and work with. Being selective implies that you are also doing something else. You are excluding certain pieces of information. You may not want to consider the romantic novels, science fiction or historical documents. You may decide you want to read and learn about the lives of famous individuals. So you turn to the section on biography and then you select a book or two or more. Now stop for a moment and go over what you have just done. What happened? You went through a search process excluding some kinds of information and including others in making your decisions.

Now flip back to a counselling session with a client. What are you doing? The same thing. You are faced with a situation where you have rapport and you want to help the client. You want the client to have power to solve his or her problems. The power you give clients is information. Information about themselves. Your counsellor role in this is to enable your clients to access useful information about themselves and to consider what they want to do with that information. The Chinese have a wonderful and wise proverb, 'If you don't know where you are going any road will do.' Often clients come for counselling because they don't know where they are going, or if they do, they don't know how to get there. They lack information. When the client can access information that is significant to them, they know the road they should be going on. From the counsellor's point of view sometimes this means going down cul-de-sacs and then coming back out of them again. On other occasions it will mean going round in a circle of enquiry only to find they come back to the same place they started at. All of this is useful for practical counselling. It informs. Einstein is reported as saying that what he enjoyed most of all was his mistakes, because he learned from them. In the same way, practical counselling should have this attitude of caring and critical enquiry. When you get stuck, when the client gets stuck, when you have 'been here before', stop and ask yourself: what have we learned? What do we know? What information do we already have that helps us to move away from this view of the situation or the problem? And when you don't have enough information, collaborate with each other about how you could find the information you need and how you will know when you find what it is you are looking for.

Practical counselling has as one of its main purposes the search for information that is relevant to clients. Armed with the appropriate counselling skills you can help clients discover just what that information is and what it specifically means to them. I have found that there are three things which can happen in getting information which you need to avoid. The first is not getting enough information about your client or their personal concerns. The second is working with too much information. And the third is not sorting out information with the client. I remember making these discoveries with clients of my own.

Here are three short examples from my own practical counselling clinics.

Insufficient Information

Sandra was 33 and wanted to lose weight. I spent some time in building rapport and, once this was achieved, I dived straight in to find out how much weight she wanted to lose, when it was a problem, and where she had control over her eating behaviour. I was sure all we had to do was identify the eating pattern, find out where there was control, and increase that span of control in different situations. Sounds simple and straightforward. Yet Sandra did not have a weight problem. Weight was only the so-called presenting problem or symptom, the secondary effect of her principal concern. I discovered later that she had a deep-seated fear of her mother and an urgent need to please her. She ate when thinking about visiting her mother. She ate when her mother visited her. She ate when her mother's letters arrived each week. And discussions at home about her mother were usually accompanied by copious cups of coffee and chocolate biscuits. It took us a long time to discover that we needed that information to make progress in our counselling sessions together.

So make sure you get enough information and of the kind which you can validate with your client. Counsellors who fail to establish sufficient information can end up in serious trouble, both for themselves and for their clients. The consequences of insufficient information can be catastrophic, and there are many disturbing examples of this.

There are two cardinal rules to follow in practical counselling. One is to actively avoid assuming you have understood the problems the clients bring to counselling when you have not. The other is to ensure you have enough information which confirms you do understand the problem and so does the client.

Information Overload

Eric, a computer analyst aged 29, came to me for counselling about his private life and problems relating to women at work. There was no stopping Eric and I encouraged him to talk. But there was no control in the counselling session. There was just too much information. Eric jumped from topic to topic. One moment he was talking about his childhood, then suddenly he was making an association with something he read in a magazine or saw on television, and wondering if "that is what is wrong with me, I heard it was hereditary, is that right?". Eric moved so rapidly from subject to subject that he never spent sufficient time on the one thing he needed to do most – limit the amount of information he was trying to manage. When he could do that, he could start to focus on examining his situation and the problems surrounding it. It turned out that Eric lived much of his life the way he approached his job. He gathered information. Lots of it. His job was a metaphor for his life. I used the metaphor of programming information as a way of enabling him to sort out the relevant information from the irrelevant, the signals from the noise. When Eric did that he made progress in his counselling sessions. He started to tidy up his life with some of the tasks I set him. And he felt better because he could achieve the goals of managing his personal information. The more in charge of 'programming' his personal information he became, the more he began to change his perceptions, attitudes and behaviour with women at work.

Information Sorting

When I apply practical counselling skills I find it is important for clients to sort out information. Sorting out information is fundamental to practical counselling. Without sorting information you end up getting nowhere with the client and they get nowhere with you. There is a story that illustrates how essential it is to sort out information when we are counselling.

One night a woman spotted a man leaning against a bright glowing street light, and looking down at the ground. She asked him what he was looking for. He said he was looking for his car keys. She asked where he had dropped them. At this point the man raised his head and turned and pointed to an area of parkland about 10 metres away from where they were both standing. Surprised at this, the woman asked him why he was looking under the street light. Without hesitation, and somewhat indignantly, the man replied, "Well it's obvious, the lighting is much better here."

This little story tells us how important it is to sort out information when we are conducting practical counselling. The immediate lesson for the counsellor is not to accept information as if it were always 'true'. The second is that we need to work from the information that the client gives us. A third lesson is that we need to find out what specific information means to the client and do an internal check at the same time on what it means to us. Finally you need to do what the woman did and ask relevant questions to find out about clients and their situation. Sorting information means asking constructive questions.

As you begin to find out what information needs to be sorted, you can help the client make sense of the situation. Sorting allows you to empower the client to get sufficient information, dispense with irrelevant information, and reduce information overload. Sorting out personal information with your clients makes it possible for you both to agree on and answer the significant question: 'What are we working with here?'

Hot and Cold Information

One last point about personal information. It is not something that is always cold and abstract. On the contrary, by definition personal information is personal. Information can be 'hot' or 'cold'. Richard Lazarus (1981), the leading psychologist on stress and coping, makes a clear distinction between the two that is useful for practical counselling. Cold information involves dealing with the facts that surround people and their problems. Where does the problem occur? Where does it occur most? In which situations does it not occur? What are you doing when the problem is present? These are all counselling questions that give us cold information. They are factual questions asking for factual answers. Questions accessing hot information are different. How do you feel when that person is present? If you could change things what would you do? What seems to be your concern? How do you know when you are going to feel this way? What would make this less of a problem for you? These questions are about the feelings and perceptions people have about their problems, what is bothering them, and what needs to be put right in their lives. Hot information is feeling and subjective. Cold information is impersonal and objective. When we are counselling clients we need to know the difference between the two kinds of information. More than this, we need to be able to know when cold information is called for and when hot information is needed. Added to this, there are times when we need to enable clients in counselling to move from one sort of information to the other, whenever the therapeutic process requires it. A brief example illustrates this point.

Sandy, a 48-year-old bachelor, came to counselling complaining about how unfortunate he was that nobody would listen to what he had to say. He said this depressed him because he could not influence any situations that were significant in his life. Lots of hot information and no cold information. The counsellor spent a valuable 20 minutes discovering useful cold information. How did he know when someone was listening to him and when they were not? What specific situations was Sandy referring to when nobody would talk to him? Did that mean there was never a time when people talked to him? What was happening now? Which specific situations were important to him and which ones were not so significant for him to influence? These were just some of the cold information questions employed in the counselling session. Once the information was gathered the counsellor could go ahead and test how hot this information was to him, what he felt when confronted with specific situations, the thoughts he had and the views he had of his feelings.

Hot information can be transformed into cold information. This can be especially useful when people come to counselling in a crisis state. You can enable them to move from their emotional state, where they are dealing with hot information, to a more composed state, where they are working with cold information. There are no hard and fast rules to follow here. However, if you want to give clients something they can use to obtain more control over themselves, moving from hot to cold information is often helpful. For example if someone says "I am just going to pieces", or "Nothing I do ever seems to work out right", or "I feel so terribly guilty about everything, I can't go on like this" you can move them into cold information so they can look at themselves more dispassionately and gain more control in the process.

Equally, cold information often needs to be converted into hot information. A lot of good practical counselling depends on transforming the cold information clients bring to counselling into hot information. People need to feel the heat of their feelings to gauge the significance of the facts they bring to counselling sessions.

Whether you are seeking to discover hot or cold information, never forget to maintain rapport. As soon as rapport is broken you need to recover it again. Remember rapport is the cement of practical counselling. It holds everything else you do together. When this is working well, clients can then begin to make new choices about themselves and how they will tackle their personal problems.

Choosing
●

Every day we make choices. Millions of them. Some of these choices we are conscious of making and others we are not. When we are not aware, we live our lives through a developed set of habits which we rely on and which get us through life more or less well, until something goes wrong.

Building rapport, accessing relevant information, managing information overload and sorting out the kinds of information that is important for clients all involve making choices. From a practical counselling perspective, I believe that clients come to counselling because the choices that they are making or not making in their lives don't work for them. Let me give you an example. A friend of mine — let's call him Steve — said he could not give up drinking. He had no control over alcohol. Alcohol controlled him and his life. Some of the consequences of this were tragic. His wife left him. His child was frightened of him and said he never wanted to see his father again. Steve also lost his job as a security guard and failed some important exams he had been studying for over five years. After some pretty heated and critical counselling sessions he came to the conclusion that he was choosing to drink, get drunk and lose control over his life. He chose to go to the pub and drink whisky. He chose to leave the house and ignore his wife and young son. He chose to solve his worries over his family and his exams by drinking even more alcohol. He chose not to turn up for work.

All he needed, he said, was to pull himself together and everything would be all right. I wonder if you have heard that one before. It was only when Steve realized he was ignoring some choices in his life and pursuing others that he began to make real progress over his problems with alcohol. It did not mean that the new choices he needed to make in his life would be easy ones.

New choices mean change and change is what practical counselling is about. New choices sometimes mean struggles. Struggles for the client and struggles for the counsellor. Clients struggle to find the resources in themselves or elsewhere to carry out the new choices that will change their situation or circumstances. The counsellor struggles to discover with the client how new choices can be identified and put into action. There are times, of course, when there is little struggle involved in making new choices. Clients simply need information on which to make the changes that are important to them.

There are also times when people seem to make choices that may have a bizarre quality about them but still have a meaning for the person making them. There's a good story that illustrates this well.

Charlie was in charge of an alligator farm in Australia where tourists flocked each holiday season. At first, it was exciting and interesting to Charlie who showed the tourists round the old swamp, the alligator lakes, the food farm and the souvenir shop. He enjoyed choosing to do this. Tourists often remarked that Charlie was genuinely interested in them and highly enthusiastic in his job. But as time went by Charlie started to get bored and became less interested in the tourists and his job. He did not want to show the tourists around or point out the alligators. He did not want to show them how each alligator had a personality of its own and each looked different from the others, Charlie's choices were 'choking him off'. Until one day, when three big bus loads of tourists arrived. He did something different. As usual, the tourists had gathered around the alligator lake for the highlight of their visit. Feeding time. But this time, suddenly and without warning, Charlie jumped into the lake. He landed right near four hungry adult alligators and had to swim for his life, just escaping with a couple of minor flesh wounds. Charlie's action created an instant mixture of great tension, amazement, excitement and relief amongst the tourists. They had never seen anyone do something like this before. Later, when he was asked why on earth he had done such a dangerous thing, Charlie said excitedly and with a renewed enthusiasm, "Aw, fair dinkum, mate, it seemed like a good idea at the time."

This story tells us a lot about choices and practical counselling. Charlie beautifully exemplifies an important point.Not all of the choices we make are wise ones! It's the same in practical counselling. Clients come to counselling for many reasons. But one of the main reasons they come is that they are unable to make new or wise choices in their lives. Or the choices they are making are unwise and have undesirable consequences for them, their families or friends. I believe counsellors should recognize that the choices their clients are making are attempts to satisfy their needs. But they do not give them what they want. There is another useful insight from Charlie and the alligators. When the choices we have been making in our lives are not working for us then it is time to try something else. Sometimes anything else. Charlie jumped in beside the alligators. It may not have been his best choice. However, it did seem better than the choices he had been making for a while. Jumping in beside the alligators helped to break up the old pattern of choices and produced a different experience for Charlie, and for the tourists. Sometimes when you are working with clients in practical counselling it will be good for them to jump in beside the alligators. Good but difficult. For choices that are sudden and dramatic can take a lot of courage. Counsellors who are prepared to work with clients on new choices and empower them to carry these choices into their lives are already courageous. To establish real and renewing change there are times when clients and counsellors need to be like Charlie with the alligators.

Choosing and Client–counsellor Outcomes

Another predominant principle of practical counselling is that we are the result of our choices. We become what we choose and we choose what we become. Choosing has consequences. So it is in choosing that clients create their outcomes for the future. Present choices create the future. What we do now affects what happens next. Sometimes the choices clients have been making up to the time they come for counselling are personally very costly. Choices that give them headaches and heartaches. Choices that lead to havoc and mayhem. Choices that ruin their careers and their marriages. Choices that they regret and wish they had never made. A great opportunity arises when clients come to practical counselling. One of the first things you can do is to ask them if they made the choice to come for counselling. If they did, you can point out to them that they have taken the first important step to changing and achieving the outcomes they need or want for their lives. In practical counselling, it is essential for the counsellor to accept that the choices clients have been making are the ones they have best available, at the time, to fulfil their needs. They may not be the 'best' choices but they are all they have got, or believe they have got, at the moment. Unfortunately, the choices that they are engaging in do not help them accomplish the sort of life they would like to lead. When I work with clients I want to find out if they know this already, and if they don't I want them to discover this for themselves. Abandoning old choices and habits is never easy. But it becomes that little bit easier for clients when they know the choices they are making, and the ones they need to keep or change.

Limited Choosing

In my view clients who come for counselling are not suffering from alcoholism, anxiety, depression, lack of self-confidence or any of the other stress-related problems. To me these are the symptoms of failing to satisfy their personal needs. Clients do come to counselling hurting, wounded and confused. There is little doubt about that. The counsellor who only addresses symptoms provides symptom relief counselling, and that can be no bad thing. However, the main thrust of practical counselling should be for the counsellor and the client to discover the underlying source of the client's personal difficulties. I have found some clients already know the answer to this question. Others take a little longer to discover it. And some seem unable to find the original moment or situation, the one where it all started. Fortunately, practical counselling does not necessarily require any client to know the precise moment or episode that started their problems. This is because practical counselling has a basic assumption about all personal problems that clients bring to counselling. It is simple, but the cornerstone of all practical counselling. Clients suffer from limited choosing, both in the past and in the present.

Clients in practical counselling therefore have a clear and specific task. It is to increase the range of choices they have available to them to manage their situation or a particular part of their life. Those carers providing practical counselling also have a clear task in relationship to the client. The counsellor's task is to find ways to influence events so that the clients can overcome their impoverished range of choices and have more choice in the way they manage their lives and their problems. The outcomes for the client and the counsellor are similar. More choices. If the client and the counsellor simply adopted the car tycoon Henry Ford's attitude of "You can have any colour you want as long as it is black", progress in counselling would be likely to come quickly to a standstill. It is up to the counsellor to use whatever ethical ways are possible to make more choices available to the client and to do what is necessary to help them discover more choices in their lives. The American psychologist Abraham Maslow was once asked by a counsellor whether it was right to use a direct or an indirect approach to helping a client. Maslow is reported to have replied immediately, "Use whatever approach is necessary." In practical counselling, the counsellor should pursue with clients new and innovative ways by which the clients can change the course of their lives. With one client, you may need to spend a great deal of time exploring a range of new choices and options, and how these could be put into practice. With another, you may have fewer options for change to choose from but you can create novel ways of making the most of these choices in specific situations that the client needs to change. I have found that this stage of counselling can come earlier or later in counselling sessions. In practical counselling you start where the client wants to start.

Tangled and Stuck — Know the Enemy

Clients who come for counselling are often tangled up and stuck. They are confused and don't know where to start. Good counselling reminds me of a famous grandmother who used to solve everyone's problems in her village. If anyone had a problem they went to see 'wise old Gran'. Problems with marriages. Problems with children. Problems with relatives. You name it, they went to Gran. Now the interesting thing about Gran was that she did a lot of knitting. She selected her own wool, spun it, made it into balls and knitted fabulous patterns. For Gran, people were like knitting. They needed to be sorted out, untangled, repatterned in their living. Gran was aware of the choices she had to make in untangling the sheep wool all the way to making it into an understandable pattern. That's why she was so good with people, wise old Gran.

Take another example. A client who comes for counselling and says, "I am angry — what are you going to do about it?" is not going to fit neatly into the counselling model that says 'that comes later'. The counsellor has to be ready to respond appropriately to the client's anger. In practical counselling this can be done with concise questioning. The concise questioning allows the counsellor to reveal the choices that underlie the anger. In this case it would be useful to ask the client "angry about what?". The counsellor could also ask the question in an angry way to reflect the tone of voice used by the client. We really need to know what it is that clients have to face in their lives. Because these are the situations that have to be dealt with now. Clearly as Baldwin (1980) found, "not everything we face can be changed, but nothing can be changed until we face it", so it is imperative to find out what the client is facing. Through rapport, information gathering and careful questioning clients can discover what it is they are facing, if they don't know already. When clients know what they are facing they have made progress in counselling. I find it helps clients if the counsellor genuinely congratulates them on identifying what it is they have to face up to. As the old Chinese proverb reminds us, "To win the battle we must first know the enemy." When clients and counsellors know the enemy they are on the same side. They fight together to defeat it in any way they know how. And when they don't succeed they need to enlist other choices, sources and resources in themselves and from others to do so.

Knowing the enemy is not enough. Practical counselling is about reality and living in the real world. However, each of us tends to have slightly different views about what is real and what matters to us. You can easily prove this for yourself. Show any group of adults a photograph of a pretty one-year-old baby. Some will say "How sweet", and they wished they had children. Others will say how they regretted having too many children. Still others will say it reminded them of their childhood and how wonderful or terrible it was. What is happening? You have demonstrated that faced with an objectively identical situation people react to it differently. They have different realities. They are alike in that they all had eyes to see the photograph and all made some comments about it. Otherwise they were different. As a psychologist once said rather cryptically, "All people are like each other some of the time, and some people are like each other all of the time but everybody is not like everyone else all of the time." Realizing this makes it imperative that counsellors work with their clients' realities and not their own. Each client may be similar to the last in a number of ways. But it would be an immense mistake for counsellors to assume that the problems clients face are all the same. On the face of it they may seem the same. But underneath, it is their problem and personal to them. One of the main contributions you can make in practical counselling is to avoid the pitfall of assuming that all clients who face similar objective situations are experiencing them in the same way.

It is one of the key tasks of practical counselling for the client and the counsellor to understand that reality and how it comes about. I say 'comes about' because we are talking about a living, breathing human being who is in the creating and the doing business. Counselling is not static and neither are the clients who come for counselling. Stuck they may be, but not static. If they are static then it is an undertaker they need, not practical counselling.

Stuck People and Awareness of Personal Choices

Stuck people come to counselling because they can't get out of life what they would like to satisfy their personal needs. They are stuck in their choices. They repeat choices that worked for them in the past but no longer work for them in the present. Or they make choices that are irresponsible and these are the very choices that create their present personal problems. The drinker, the person who batters his wife, the child abuser, are all making choices that have regrettable consequences for themselves and damaging effects on those who are associated with them. Unless the client's choice repertoire is enlarged, these patterns of behaviour will tend to repeat themselves more or less frequently in the future. Some choices need to be extended, others reduced, and others erased from the way they behave, think and feel.

Our past choices not only bring us to where we are in the present, they create our futures as well. When I am working with clients within a practical counselling framework, one of the first things I like to find out is just how much they are aware of the choices they are making in their lives. Often they are unaware of their personal choices. Clients have to become more aware of the personal choices they make and the consequences they are having. It is the counsellor who facilitates this process and helps the client discover the significance of these choices. With rapport, information, and awareness of their personal choices they can start to realize why they are stuck, what makes them stuck, and what they might do about becoming unstuck from their problems. The counsellor has the task of creating the conditions in counselling where clients can begin to unglue themselves and become more flexible in choosing how they run their lives.

Flexibility and Personal Outcomes

The people I see for counselling are all different in their own special way but they all have one thing in common. The solutions they have attempted to use to solve their personal problems and concerns don't work for them. In other words the choices they have been making and putting into action are not satisfying their needs or achieving their goals. Their thoughts, feelings and behaviours are not flexible enough to affect their personal

outcomes. One of the first things to find out in practical counselling is what clients have been doing that has not given them
sufficient satisfaction in their lives. The man who is drinking to
forget his divorce; the woman who continues to live with a man
who batters her, in return for financial security; the adolescent
who is bullied at school and buys favours from his friends in an
attempt to be liked — these are all examples of people making
choices to satisfy their personal needs, choices that solve problems at the expense of creating others.

Initially, it is helpful to clients to learn what it is they are doing
in these situations and to appreciate the consequences their
actions are having for themselves and others. So one of the first
things to do in practical counselling is to show clients the way
that they have been trying to solve their problems and the results
this produces. When this has been done you can venture to find
out if this is satisfying to the client. Most of the time it will not
be. Otherwise they would not have come for counselling, unless
they were coerced by someone else, and if they have been you
need to find out who really has the problem, and who it is that
requires counselling.

Reaching the point where the counsellor and the client agree
that the way the client is trying to satisfy his or her needs is not
appropriate is a crucial point in counselling. It creates the opportunity, for the counsellor and the client, of introducing change
and more flexibility in the tasks they have to work on together.
When it happens, be sure to congratulate your clients on this
realization. You can also congratulate them on wanting to try
something else. Coming to counselling is the first step in trying
something different. Something the client has not tried before. I
have found that clients need to be more flexible in their approach
to their lives, their personal problems and the way in which they
try to solve them. Congratulating clients on coming to counselling, congratulating them on realizing they need to change,
congratulating them on being prepared to try new ways of solving their problems, helps clients. It helps them to challenge their
perceptions of themselves as failures and doing the 'wrong' things
in their lives, and gain perceptions of themselves as starting to
tackle their problems in fresh ways that create the motivation for
changing their futures.

Sometimes clients are so well-rehearsed in 'telling their story' that counsellors seem to be getting nowhere with them. This can go on for many sessions. It is not the client's fault and it's not the counsellor's either. In these instances, clients have usually been to see lots of other carers. By the time they get to counselling they have a view of their problem and how it affects them. Some even have acquired many of the names and diagnoses you find in psychiatry textbooks. One man I was helping spent the first session talking to me in jargon about his complexes and how his main problem was a pathological attachment to his mother based on an unsatisfactory Oedipal urge. We quickly discovered our first task: to talk to each other and understand each other.

In situations like this I like to surprise clients and take them away from choosing to play the same old story over and over again. I find distraction is very effective. In the middle of their telling me their story I might ask them to tell me what they know about plasticine. This often stops everything. And this is what is intended. I want them to get the opportunity of understanding how their choices are blocking any progress they would like to make in their lives. Even when clients sound incredulous and query what I have asked them, I persist and say, "Yes, tell me what you know about plasticine." They then tell me, "It's something you can put into shapes, children play with it, it comes in different colours, you can stretch it and you can try out blending different shapes and colours together ..." and so on. I then sometimes comment, "Isn't it interesting how you can do all of these things with plasticine." I then ask what you can do with concrete. They say things like, "It is a mixture of things that you use for holding things together or holding buildings up or anything that has to do with setting and securing and making strong, and it sets hard." I ask them then to let me know if they notice any similarities or differences between plasticine and concrete and their problems. For the first time clients don't restart telling their story or their problems where they left off. Instead they come back with observations about themselves such as "I am set like the concrete"; "I have the wrong mixture of things in my life. I need to put these right"; "I am being too hard on myself"; "I am like the concrete in one way because I am fixed in the way I have been going about solving my problems, I need to be more like the plasticine, try putting myself into a different shape"; "I need to stretch myself a bit and put more colours in my life"; "I definitely need to learn to become less serious about everything and play, play with some new choices or at least try them out."

I am not saying you need to do this with every client who comes for counselling. However, when clients are stuck and are well-rehearsed in telling you about their problems, it is often very helpful to use distraction methods such as those I have mentioned. As a general rule of thumb, use distraction or other means of surprise when your clients seem to be stuck, repeat themselves, or have a well-established view of themselves, their problems, and why they are the way they say they are. Remember practical counselling is about influencing. Influencing with integrity. Many times, in practical counselling, you will find your task is to enable your clients to try something else, something else that will change their situation or the way they see themselves, even in some small way.

When you are faced with clients who need help to break up their patterns of choices and discover new ones to put into practice in their lives just remember the conversation the White Queen and Alice had in Lewis Carroll's *Through the Looking Glass:*

"I can't believe that!" said Alice.

"Can't you?" the Queen said in a pitying tone. "Try again: draw a long breath, and shut your eyes."

Alice laughed. "There's no use trying," she said: "One *can't* believe impossible things."

"I daresay you haven't had much practice," said the Queen. "When I was your age, I always did it for half-an-hour a day. Why, sometimes I've believed as many as six impossible things before breakfast."

Maybe she did not know it but the White Queen was doing a good job of practical counselling with Alice. When clients believe things that stop them from achieving their goals they need to change. Clients need to start believing they can change. When they do believe they can make and create new choices for themselves, they can start trying to find new ways of solving their problems, and overcoming their personal pain. Putting trying into practice is a big step forward for clients. The first steps may be faltering. Sometimes clients need to 'learn to walk' all over again. Others simply have to learn to find out where their feet are taking them and change course. However all clients, in my experience, need to have three things if they are to make further progress in counselling. First, they need to believe they can change themselves or their situation. Second, they need to want to try something different from the way they have been trying to solve their problems up to the present. Third and essential, they should be putting into practice the new choices they have selected to change their lives to a greater or lesser extent.

Personal Outcomes and Change

Clearly, practical counselling with clients is greatly enhanced when you know which personal outcomes you are aiming for. It's a great waste of effort if you don't know the outcomes you need to achieve in counselling. This applies to both the counsellor and the client. Just recall for a moment the effort put into a typical counselling session. You work at building rapport. You work at accessing relevant information. You are flexible in the approaches taken with each client. The clients are the same. They reciprocate. They are willing to explore, examine and sort out hot and cold information that is significant to them. They too are prepared to be flexible to get out of their rut. There is just one problem. Neither you nor the client know what outcomes you are aiming for in counselling. What do you do? You need to know where the goalposts are in order to reach your goals. Some people may argue that personal outcomes are just the same as personal goals. I take a different view. For me personal outcomes mean more to individuals, couples and families. They are bigger than goals. Buckminster Fuller, one of the greatest thinkers this century, describes this as the 'law of precession'. Seen in this way, personal outcomes embrace the goal setting process and more. Attaining personal outcomes ensures that clients gain other things in addition to their goals.

Getting a new job; filing for divorce; kicking the cocaine habit; learning to fly; increasing your income by £10,000 per year; paying off your mortgage by the time you are 55; saying "please" when you want to borrow your friend's car — these can all be personal goals. However, in pursuing them, clients can enrich their experience, develop persistence, find new courage, overcome frustration and discover personal powers of concentration, confidence and disciplined responsibility. This is the stuff of personal outcomes. So personal outcomes are not just about goals and goal setting. They are about the process of personal development that clients undergo in the pursuit of their goals. Personal outcomes are about clients knowing where they want to be and how they are going to get there. But of at least equal importance is what they become along the way. It is very likely that clients will gain a fresh perspective of themselves and experience new learning and personal growth as a result of their counselling sessions.

Working with personal outcomes can be important throughout our counselling sessions. Whether at the beginning, during, or at the conclusion of a counselling session, clients and counsellors need to decide where they are and where they are trying to get to. This situation often changes. It can change between counselling sessions. It can change within each counselling session, as you make progress with clients. Personal outcomes are like living things. What we want and need can change between breakfast and dinner or stay the same for years. The point for counsellors as I see it is for them to be aware of their own personal outcomes and those of their clients as they relate to each counselling session.

I am not suggesting that clients or counsellors regularly fail to pay attention to making their personal outcomes in counselling explicit. However, it can happen. When it does, everybody loses. You don't know what the clients really want for themselves from counselling sessions. They don't know what you want either. When neither the counsellor nor the client knows what their personal outcomes are for counselling they should, as far as possible, make them known to each other.

I find this is important for a number of reasons. First, unless personal outcomes are made explicit in practical counselling, it can lead to misunderstanding between the client and counsellor. The client may have one set of personal outcomes and the counsellor another. When I practise practical counselling, I make it clear what my personal outcomes are for the sessions I have with clients. I tell them my outcomes are to work with them, so long as they agree, to find out what it is they need or want and how they might go about achieving it. If you do happen to have difficulty in establishing personal outcomes in counselling, you need to maintain rapport and go back and get more information from the client.

Other personal outcomes that can be brought into play as counselling progresses can involve:

1   Speeding up or slowing down the pace of counselling;
2   Setting tasks for clients;
3   Rehearsing solutions to problems when clients say they can't do something they want to, adopting a 'let's pretend we can' approach;
4   Refusing to take action unless the client is really ready to, creating a climate for change;
5   Asking clients for help, inviting them to tell you the best way you could help them at the moment.

There are many, many, more personal outcomes that I bring into play during counselling sessions with clients. Each depends on the particular client and the stage of counselling we seem to be at. However, more important than anything, is for the counsellor to be aware of the client's personal outcomes for counselling. If client outcomes are opposed to those of the counsellor or in some direct conflict with them, then the counsellor needs to amend or abandon his or her personal outcomes. The personal outcomes of the counsellor should never get in the way of the clients or what they seek to accomplish. Where the personal outcomes of the counsellor really score and can be introduced is in the service of the client.

As one experienced counsellor put it, "When I know what you want, then I know what you need. And when I know that you know I know what your personal outcomes are, I can align my personal outcomes to achieve yours." Aligning your personal outcomes with those of the clients makes for more effective counselling.

Reviewing, Resourcing and Releasing
●

Reviewing the present position with the client helps to establish how far counselling has progressed since you started counselling sessions. Reviewing also does something else. It makes it possible for clients to take another look at where they have come from and where they are now. Reviewing helps the counsellor and the client. It helps the counsellor to 'check out' with the client whether change has occurred or if indeed the client prefers not to change at present. It helps the client to 'see, hear and feel' where they are and experience support from the counsellor.

You can imagine reviewing being like the activity of those radar operators you see in old films aboard submarines. They regularly inspect their radar screens just to make sure the submarine is heading in the right direction or whether they may be heading for troubled waters. As a counsellor you are like the radar operator. You keep your 'antennae' tuned into your clients so you can give them a view of their situation as it develops and as they make progress on their journey in counselling. Sometimes you will be giving them 'full speed ahead' signals, sometimes 'slow down'. Sometimes you may even have to steer them away from danger or face it straight and head on. Much depends on your judgement of the resources your clients have at their disposal. Reviewing also allows clients and counsellors to decide just how much more work has to be done in and outside counselling sessions to bring about the future changes clients want for themselves. Another purpose of reviewing is to feed back to the client the successes they have had since counselling began.

Change requires resources. These resources are potentially available to the client from three directions: themselves, the counsellor, and people outside the counselling session. These resources can be highly personal to the client. They may be resources they can access one at a time, in part or some combination of all three at once. What is essential for effective counselling is that the client should have access to resources of some sort. It doesn't really matter whether it is from themselves, or their counsellor, or someone else. These are academic issues. Practically, clients need to have access to resources they can utilize to challenge, manage and overcome problems that concern them. It's the counsellor's job to enable the client to discover these resources.

In some instances, you merely have to point to resources that clients already have but that they do not realize they have readily available to them. For example, a client of mine, a 36-year-old self-employed man, was unable to tell his wife how much he loved her. Let's call them Phil and Jenny. Phil and Jenny said they were strangers. Phil spent a great deal of time away from home. Jenny had developed a love–hate relationship to Phil and the inordinate amount of time he spent in the business. Phil had spent so much time building up his road haulage business that he seemed to forget how very important Jenny was to him. Phil and Jenny both came to me. They spent the session together rowing and blaming each other. They said they could not communicate. I asked them what it was about them that they cared so much about their situation that they were prepared to row about it. They came to the same conclusion. They still loved each other. The problem was that they did not know how to get that 'old feeling' back again. After some time they discovered where they might find it. When they first started the haulage company Jenny was secretary and confidante to Phil and Phil relied on Jenny a great deal. That gradually faded away as the company grew. Our session ended with my setting a task for Phil and Jenny. I said, "I want you to go away this weekend. I want you to go down memory lane, and no ifs, ands or buts, OK ... OK ... Go back to where you first met. Go back to the time you got your first office together. Get out the photograph album and do one more thing. Relive all of those experiences you had just as if they were happening again." This is a very brief summary of how the tasks I set Phil and Jenny came about. So what happened?

Phil and Jenny came for another counselling session 10 days later. Both looked different and they were comfortable in each other's company. They talked and talked about all of the things they had rediscovered in themselves and the plans they were starting to make for the future. Some of these involved visiting relatives they had not seen for years. Other plans were more ambitious: a second honeymoon, Jenny joining the business again. I was pleasantly surprised, but not as much as they were. Somehow they had rediscovered those feelings about each other — the ones that brought new life back into their relationship. My contribution was to give them a route to accessing those feelings that they said they both wanted. They did the rest.

Practical counselling involves being non-directive at times and at others becoming quite directive. Both approaches, however, should be guided by everyone releasing the necessary resources to achieve their personal outcomes.

Releasing resources for personal change is well illustrated by this story. Mark Twain's characters Tom Sawyer and Huckleberry Finn are rumoured to have been based on real people. In those pioneering days when people had to find their way across uncharted lands, the children used to make their own fun and games. One of the favourites was dam-making and dam-busting. The kids got the idea from watching how beavers worked away at storing up water for their survival. The kids weren't as good at it as the beavers but they soon learned how to make 'a darn good dam'. Now some of these dams would be protected by the kids. Because the idea was for the other kids to go dam-busting. When the dams were bust the water would come surging out in a great flood of energy and the kids would go scampering across it shouting, "Gotcha, gotcha, gotcha dam-bust". As time went by some of these kids got wiser and built little tributaries that redirected the water when a dam-bust raid broke the banks of the dam. For the kids it was great fun. But it sometimes made them angry and anxious to protect their dam. Most of all they learned how to build better dams and how to deal with dam-busts when they took place.

Counsellors who work with practical counselling remind me of those dam-busters and dam-building kids. Releasing resources in practical counselling can be like releasing surges of personal energy in clients. Counsellors may help clients to release their personal resources in a great surge, a torrent of feelings and unrestrained emotions. They can also make it possible for clients to redirect their energies and to build new ways of living their lives. And when clients know which direction they want to take themselves, they can learn how to let their new-found energies flow and find new levels of meaning for themselves. Practical counselling helps clients to break away from those things that hold them back from changing themselves or their situation. It also permits clients to have the opportunity of rebuilding and restoring their lives and the way they want to live in the future.

Overview

●

Practical counselling is about influencing with integrity. The counsellor is involved with clients in attempts to influence events so that clients can accomplish the personal outcomes that are significant in their lives. To do this we need to build rapport with our clients and maintain that rapport throughout our contact with clients who come for counselling. Rapport provides the basis for affording clients access to information and enabling them to examine that information in a way that is personally meaningful. With the critical but caring support of the counsellor, clients can sort through their information. They can examine it, question it, evaluate it and decide which information is important for them to work on and what should be disregarded. Further progress in practical counselling comes with clients making choices about how they want to change their lives and what their personal outcomes are for themselves. Here the counsellor helps clients to move away from rigid patterns and limited choices towards being more flexible and enlarging the range of choices they have to overcome their problems and see how these might be put into practice. Periodically, counsellors should review how well their clients are doing and consider with them the kinds of resources they need and how these can be released so they can gain control over their problems and live fuller and more rewarding lives.

You can't step twice into the same river
HERACLITUS
*I don't think the therapist does anything except provide the
opportunity to think about your problem in a favourable climate*
MILTON H ERICKSON

Chapter 2

CREATING THE CONDITIONS FOR CHANGE

Clients, Counsellors and Change
●

Clients usually come to counselling because something has to be changed. The client does not always know what that something is, especially early on in counselling sessions. In addition to this, the counsellor rarely knows what clients need to change in themselves or their situation. And even if they do know, it is nearly always unhelpful simply to tell clients what they need to do to sort out their problems. It is one of the tasks of the counsellor to enable clients to find out what it is they need to talk about and that takes time. As clients discover what it is they want to talk about in counselling, so the counsellor begins to find out what it is that is important for the clients. So one of the first things that clients and counsellors do early in counselling, and in succeeding counselling sessions, is to go through a process of 'prospecting', looking for the things that need to be brought into counselling. Sometimes these may seem trivial at first, but later they may turn out to be especially important to the client. At this stage of counselling, the counsellor and the client collaborate with each other in identifying what the problems are and formulating what it is they need to work on together. Clearly, rapport has to be established early and the counsellor spends time listening to the client's view of the difficulties, and what the client has done so far to overcome the problems. I find it is also useful to explore with clients what the outcomes of their attempts have been to solve their problems and what lessons they have learned so far.

One of the counsellor's main goals in practical counselling is to create the conditions where clients can change. Change comes in many shapes and forms. Clients can change the way they think about their problems. They can change the way they feel about their problems, and they can change the way they behave in situations associated with their problems. Another change they may choose to make is not to try to do anything about the problems that they bring to counselling. Changing from trying to solve problems in their personal lives to letting the problems work themselves out has brought significant changes in clients. When clients choose to stop trying it is still a change for them. Such changes should not be underestimated for their therapeutic or healing value. The essential point is that for counselling to have a real and lasting effect, clients should be free to choose the changes they wish to make in their lives. Equally, counsellors can influence the counselling process in any ethical way they can with the intention of making more choices available to clients. These choices are the basis on which clients can then consider, and make decisions about, what it is they need to change in themselves, others, or their situation.

Trust and Respect
The Core of Counselling

●

Clients are unlikely to want to make any changes unless they trust and respect the counsellor. Change can be seriously obstructed unless there is a strong bond of this kind between the client and the counsellor. It is a truism among counsellors that if you lose a client's trust and respect, you have lost the battle for change with the client. Whatever form of practical counselling you are offering to clients, you need to ensure that you create a climate of trust and respect during counselling sessions. Carl Rogers, the founder of person-centred counselling, held the view that trusting in the potential of the client and respecting them lay at the core of counselling. He believed the counsellor should convey "... respect and full acceptance of the client as he/she is and similar attitudes towards the client's potentialities for dealing with his/her situations ..." (1986). Also, if the counsellor expresses attitudes of full acceptance and a deep respect towards clients, both for their problems and their potentialities to solve their problems, within a climate of warmth and genuineness, the conditions for change are more likely to be created.

Trust and respect are reciprocal in practical counselling. The give and take between you and the client provides opportunities for mutuality, a respect for each other. Implicit in the relationship between the counsellor and the client is the belief that together you have the capacity and competence to explore and to understand each other. Further than this, clients should come to the point where they realize that you respect and trust their potential for resolving their own problems. This is one of the main influencing roles that the counsellor plays during practical counselling.

Clearly, trust and respect need to be conveyed by the counsellor towards clients at the start of counselling and throughout their contact with clients. However, making sure you generate trust and respect does not mean you will always agree with the client's thoughts, feelings or behaviour. Simply agreeing with your clients may only serve to maintain their problems and hold up any changes they would like to make. Nevertheless, early on in counselling sessions, when you are building rapport and gathering information, it is important to acknowledge what clients are saying and to clarify with them from time to time that you understand what they are saying and meaning when they are telling you about their personal problems. However, acknowledging the client should not be construed as endorsing agreement, and you should be vigilant to make sure this difference is observed in counselling sessions.

Trusting and Client Confidentiality

Trusting and respecting the client are useful for building rapport with clients. In turn, clients often develop trust and respect and are protective of their relationships with their counsellors. Trust and respect can be built. Sometimes it has to be earned by counsellors and clients. Occasionally there is no easy road to building trust or respect, especially when some clients have been disappointed or 'let down' in their previous relationships with others. Achieving trust and respect can sometimes be a fragile beginning in counselling for counsellors and clients.

Establishing and maintaining a climate of confidentiality between yourself and clients greatly helps to strengthen trust and respect. In practical counselling the client's trust of the counsellor should never be broken. The counsellor is the guardian of the client's privacy. Client confidentiality is the responsibility of the counsellor and should be maintained within a strict and clear code of professional practice. If, or when, confidentiality is breached, it should be for reasons that both the client and the counsellor understand and have previously agreed to. There are good practical, therapeutic and ethical reasons for establishing and maintaining client confidentiality in counselling. They act as golden guidelines for counsellors offering practical counselling. It pays to keep them in mind when you are working with clients. (See *Guidelines for Maintaining Client Confidentiality*, page 34.)

Hearing and Being Heard

●

When the conditions of trust and confidentiality are created, client change can begin to take place. One of the essentials of conducting counselling sessions is for clients to know they are being heard and for counsellors to understand that they are hearing the client. Hearing is a special kind of listening. It involves being able to appreciate at a deep level what it is like for clients at that particular time and over time as they express their concerns to you.

Hearing the client does not mean being ready to intervene and give advice. In my experience, this kind of listening blocks progress in counselling. Counselling is not an advice-giving activity. Moreover, giving advice — even with the most genuine of intentions — often only serves to frustrate clients and make them angry. It can also damage any rapport building and seal off attempts by the counsellor to access information of importance to the client. Counsellors who are not hearing what the client is saying, thinking, feeling or doing are not 'with' the client. In such instances, the client may adopt the attitude, 'If you are not hearing what I am saying, then I have nothing for you to hear.' At worst they may drop out of counselling and simply refuse to turn up for counselling sessions.

Look out for those tell-tale signs that you have not quite heard the client. They come in little episodes such as the client saying,

Guidelines for Maintaining Client Confidentiality

1 Take every reasonable precaution to preserve the confidentiality of information acquired throughout your contact with clients.

2 Make it your practice to protect the identity and privacy of clients except in those cases where you are subject to the requirements of the law or you have the expressed permission of clients to reveal their identity to others.

3 Ensure that colleagues and other staff or trainees with whom you work are also aware of the need to maintain client confidentiality and that they respect this with each individual they directly or indirectly associate with in counselling.

4 When you do communicate information about your practice or your research in counselling, make every endeavour to protect the identity of clients associated with it.

5 Safeguard any records you keep about clients, whether written or stored in computer systems.

6 At the outset of counselling, make clear to clients the rights they have about accessing the information you hold about them.

7 Where there is evidence and a compelling reason to breach confidentiality, as with the admission of a serious crime, clients should be made aware of their position and the appropriate third parties informed.

8 The recording of counselling sessions by audio, video, photographic or other electro-reproductive means should only be conducted with the prior and expressed agreement of clients.

9 In any demonstration of counselling skills or public work with clients you should ensure you obtain their written permission and specify the conditions under which such sessions should take place.

10 Take all reasonable steps to ensure that the client records over which you have control only exist for as long as it is necessary to identify individuals. Thereafter records should be either destroyed, given back to clients, or rendered anonymous so as to make it impossible to identify clients.

"No you haven't understood what I am saying", "No that is not-what I mean", or "You are quite wrong, everybody else thinks that as well, that's not what is bothering me." Even when this happens, and it does happen even when every effort is being made to hear what it is clients need us to hear, we can utilize the clients' concerns by asking them what it is they do mean and return to listening carefully to what they are trying to communicate during counselling sessions.

One of the most difficult situations that can arise is where both the client and the counsellor are not hearing each other or being heard. In this situation, the client and the counsellor can become confused and uncomfortable with each other. The exchange of information between the client and the counsellor may become distorted and the client's views misrepresented by the carer providing counselling. Not hearing or being heard can also lead clients to wonder why they are attending counselling sessions or even to stop coming to the sessions. Conversely, the counsellor, not hearing or being heard by the client, can also run the risk of prematurely terminating the number of counselling sessions with the client. Clearly, hearing and being heard needs to be mutual, and established, maintained and nurtured throughout the counsellor's contact with clients. It is a two-way process. Through actively listening to each other the client and the counsellor can hear each other and be heard.

Hearing and being heard opens up counselling and new possibilities for the client. It liberates the counsellor and the client from the prison of their mindsets, conditioned reactions, preconceived ideas, judgements and opinions. It puts clients in touch with personal resources they thought they never had, that have not been used for some time or that the clients had simply forgotten about until now. Very often, these are the personal resources which counsellors can accept and utilize with clients as the point from which to begin to move from their present 'problem' position. Personal change frequently occurs for clients when they know they have been heard in counselling. They can then also start to hear themselves, what they need, and how they might satisfy their needs in different ways in the future. Hearing and being heard involves a special kind of listening in counselling: careful listening.

Careful Listening

Careful listening is necessary with clients in counselling. This involves conducting counselling sessions with an attitude of care and alertness towards what clients are saying. Time and time again counsellors say they 'just listened' to their clients. Clients often say they were 'listened to for the first time', and 'at last someone understands my problem'. Careful listening is non-judgemental. It is not an attempt to get the information that the counsellor is interested in and then jump to a diagnostic conclusion about clients. Careful listening has two parts to it. First of all you have to take care to attend painstakingly to what clients are saying, and be cautious and restrained in pushing clients in any direction other than the one they seem to be taking at the time. Second, you really have to listen to what your clients say, how they say it, and the personal meanings they attach to their communications about themselves and others. In counselling terms, you need to 'hear' the person who is your client.

To be able to hear people means you have to be good at listening to them. Hearing means careful listening to the words they say and what they mean. Yet it is even more than this. It also means listening for and hearing the thoughts behind the words and the feelings and tonality used by clients to describe the personal meanings they give to their world, their reality, and their situation.

Sometimes listening in this way quickly reveals the real problems the client faces and needs to tackle. At other times, it will mean listening for the message within the message: the deep human cry for help that lies trapped in their messages of pain. When you can listen and hear, and when clients realize they are being listened to and being heard, a wonderful thing can start to happen. The seeds of change begin to grow, and perhaps for the first time clients feel fresh hope for themselves and their futures. For when clients know you hear them, they can then begin to listen to themselves. And when they can listen to themselves in the safety and security of the counselling sessions, they can begin to consider what their real problems are, who or what is responsible for them, and what are their options for the future. If I have found anything in providing practical counselling to clients, it is this:

careful listening to clients very often creates hope for the future, because it implies that we care for the client and caring for the client creates hope.

Timing and Feedback

•

Hope is a great motivator for clients. Therefore, it is important that the hope of change is strengthened and not weakened by the counsellor. I have found there is a great temptation in counselling clients to try to do too much too soon. The waves of caring that come when a client shows trust, and the conditions of confidentiality have been satisfied, sometimes lead counsellors to try to nudge the change process along. There are times when this can be no bad thing. For instance when a client continually tells the same story at counselling sessions, the counsellor needs to use a more direct approach to changing the course of counselling or to find out what need the repetition of the same story is fulfilling for the client. I think it essential for counsellors to acknowledge that their clients may not have the personal skills to break the cycle of behaviour they have got into. It is therefore a responsibility of the counsellor to lead the client into confronting what is going on, with the intention of changing it.

However, this is a question of judgement on the part of who-ever is providing the counselling sessions. I find it helpful frequently to ask myself whether the time is right to encourage clients to examine or explore specific problems or go straight for making pragmatic changes in their lives. Here counsellors need to ask themselves, and indeed sometimes discuss with others, a very serious question. How does the counsellor know when to work with clients on certain areas of their lives and problems and not others? There is no easy answer to this question. However, when you are fully listening to your clients and hearing what they say, you will be able to improve your ability to pick out what it is that is really bothering them and what they really need to work on. Some clients will make this very clear from the start of your contact with them. Others take more time to formulate what it is they are concerned about and what it is they could be doing about it. As a very general rule the counsellor should be guided by the client. It is feedback from the client that tells the counsellor where they should be going next in their sessions.

In no way does this suggest that you have stopped influencing during counselling sessions. What it does mean is that the client and the counsellor are counter-influencing each other. Once you know what it is that clients need to deal with, you can move with them into exploring it and how it might be changed.

You might find it helpful to think of the analogy of driving a car. You don't just jump in your car, switch on the ignition and accelerate, hoping everything will work out right. You probably take into account the road conditions, other vehicles, the kind of traffic flow, your speed, direction and control over your use of the road. And how do you do that? You use feedback, and feedback provides you with the basis for making decisions and choices about what you do next during driving. The more inexperienced the driver, the more care and time are needed to consciously make decisions. The more experienced and proficient the driver, the less time is needed to make decisions, and sometimes these are made so rapidly they are done at an unconscious level of awareness.

Counselling is similar. Knowing when to ask questions and when to let the clients do the talking; knowing when to check that you have understood them; knowing when clients need to look at themselves from a different viewpoint; knowing when to be direct and confrontational and when to be less directive and supportive all rely on feedback from the client. Feedback is information. And the counsellor has to be sensitive to the information that the client is sending back in their counselling sessions. Sometimes the signals will be clear and unambiguous; at others they need clarifying, amplifying and interpreting, so that doubt about what to do next is reduced. Having relevant information of this kind helps the counsellor to help the client. One further point about feedback. In practical counselling, clients don't always know the kind of information that the counsellor needs to help them. So it is important that you are as vigilant about the feedback you are not getting from clients as about that which you are getting. Let me give you an example.

Bernard, a 37-year-old married man with two children, came to see me recently for counselling. He started off by telling me he already knew what his problem was and that all he needed to do was to clarify how he could improve himself. He said he was over-working and all he needed to do was to manage his time better so he could "go to work and get home at a reasonable hour like other people".

He said he thought, "we could get this sorted out in one session". However, because I did not know if this was simply the case I needed more information. Information that the present feedback from Bernard did not provide. Further into the counselling session we discovered that, although Bernard did work very hard, it appeared he did not need to. Also it was evident he liked making decisions and was a leader at work. It was characteristic that he had told me how long the counselling session was going to take and what the problem was. Eventually, in subsequent counselling sessions Bernard started to talk about his family life and how his wife was in charge at home and he had no say in how things were run at home. It was then and only then that he spoke with a voice of sudden realization, filled with angry feelings, saying that he now knew his real problem was not over-work but escaping from home. It turned out Bernard wanted to have more say at home and to improve his relationship with his wife. We had now identified the real problem that he wanted to work on.

Taking Stock

●

Recognizing the real problem often means engaging with clients in a process of taking stock of their situation and getting a clear overview of it. Taking stock, and periodically summarizing where the client is at each counselling session, helps both client and counsellor to keep a watchful eye on any progress or pitfalls that remain to be resolved. I like the analogy of taking stock and summarizing the state of the store. It simply but elegantly conveys the essence of taking stock and summarizing skills in practical counselling.

Anyone who has ever been into a large high street store like Marks and Spencer can't fail to be impressed by the large range of goods in stock for sale. The stocks of goods are a statement of the availability of items and they are also a summary of the current state of what is in the store. We could tell from past inventories what was stocked, what sold, what was reordered and what was not, and what plans for future stocks are being made. Finally, a summary of items can be made and stored for future use. This is in some ways very close to what happens in counselling sessions.

You need periodically to take stock with the client and summarize the past, present or future situation as the client sees it. In this way counsellors can enable clients to take stock of the abilities they have and resources they may need to strengthen their hopes for changing their situation now or in the future. Summarizing in practical counselling is a way of saying to the client, "We have done a stock-take and this is the state of the store."

The store is the present range of resources that clients have immediately available to them to work with in their situation. Or it may mean drawing attention to personal capabilities clients have long forgotten they had, but which they could use to change something in themselves or their situation. Alternatively, you can help clients simply to take stock of what goals are important to them without necessarily emphasizing any need for immediate action or change. After all, anybody can visit a store and can look without having to buy anything. A case example shows how clients can benefit from counsellors using this set of counselling skills.

Ramon was 39, divorced, and living with his mother, who had been widowed three months before.

RAMON: You don't know what it's like, every day the same old routine ... every single day ... get up, make her breakfast ... And you know what, I keep doing it ...

COUNSELLOR *(showing interest and listening, but encouraging Ramon to go on):* Mm ... you keep doing it ...

RAMON: Yeh, I mean I have my job at the factory. The shifts put a lot of pressure on me and, well, I get tired and angry ... It's all right for Mum, she's relied on me, I suppose, since Dad died. Yet I just wanted to help out, I didn't think I would ever move back in again. It's no use, I can't take anyone back home, friends or girlfriends, well she doesn't like it. Sure, it's her place, but I have had enough. Everybody says I ought to have it out with Mum, but she is heartbroken. I can't do that to her ... You see it is hopeless, it's a hopeless mess. I don't know how to get out of it. I mean if I leave now

Mum won't have any support from me, and my sister will write to me from Australia telling me what a pig I have been. It will just add to Mum's distress ... But, well, at the same time, if I stay I will just get angrier and ... I hope Mum doesn't think I am back for good or making up for Dad not being there any more.

COUNSELLOR *(now feeds back to Ramon, summarizing and inviting him to take stock):* Ramon, as I have been sitting here listening to you, it seems to me that you are saying that since a personal tragedy occurred to your mother you have been helping her and supporting her. Yet at the same time this is costing you some of your freedom to live your own life and that you do have other responsibilities and choices you would like to pursue ... However, you are not quite sure how you can change your situation at present ... and that this could cause you more concern about your relationship with your mum. And I am ... wondering if any of what I am saying just now makes sense to you?

RAMON: Sure, a lot of it makes sense ... But not all of it ... I mean the bit about my concern about my mum ... well, I think she might be able to look after herself. But I do know one thing for sure ... I can see I have got myself into a terrible situation ... I need ... I need ...

COUNSELLOR: You need to ... *(Inviting Ramon to say what this taking stock has meant to him)*

RAMON: I need to look at what I can do about it ... don't I?

COUNSELLOR: That is something we can work on together, if you would like to, Ramon.

You may have noticed how careful the counsellor was not to push Ramon into making emotional outbursts about his mother, and not to take a dismissive attitude towards him or his sister. Summarizing the situation enables Ramon to take stock of what he is saying and what he really means by it. It also allows both the counsellor and the client to check with each other that they are hearing the same thing. In other words the counsellor goes at the pace of the client. Another reason for going at the pace of the client is to give him or her the opportunity of disagreeing with the counsellor's summary of what has been heard. When clients disagree with you, it is important not to take it personally. If you do, you can run a very high risk of sabotaging any therapeutic gains you might have made to date as a result of counselling.

Moreover, when a client disagrees with a counsellor, it may be the first time they have felt safe enough to assert themselves in any way.

Taking stock and offering a summary to the client achieves two other goals. It helps to maintain rapport and direction during counselling. It also empowers the client to make changes and some of these changes may involve disagreeing with the summaries offered during counselling.

Indeed, in the particular case example we have just examined, it was of paramount importance for Ramon not to agree wholeheartedly with the counsellor. It became clear even early on in counselling that he confused his guilt and loyalty to his mother and anger at his sister with his own needs. It turned out in later counselling sessions that Ramon had been dominated by women throughout his life, especially by his sister and mother. So when your clients disagree with your summaries or they take stock and see things differently from you, learn to accept this as an interesting opportunity to explore territory further with them. You are not your clients' keeper.

Self-disclosing in Counselling Sessions

●

Studies of effective practical counselling show that clients often disclose details of their personal lives to counsellors that they have never shared with anyone else. This does not come about by accident. Consider a typical counselling situation for a moment. You talk to your clients, and they talk to you. You establish rapport and you begin to access information. How do they see their problem? How long has it lasted? When was the last time they experienced this difficulty? What specifically have they done to try to overcome their troubles? What results did this have for them and others? Now, some clients may be prepared to disclose all of this information about themselves. But people are not machines. They have opinions, values and a right to privacy. Most of all, clients should never feel they are being interrogated by their counsellors. Unfortunately, sometimes newly fledged counsellors or those keen to use counselling skills in their work fall into this trap. How can this be avoided?

Avoiding the trap rests in being able to recognize and acknowledge that counselling is a two-way process. It is essential that counsellors develop the skill of disclosing aspects of themselves to their clients. When counsellors let clients into their lives, clients tend to reciprocate. This sharing of aspects of ourselves with others in counselling facilitates a climate of care and share, where client and counsellor define a special place and occasions where they can allow parts of themselves to make contact with each other.

Using the skill of self-disclosure, the counsellor provides a role model for the client to follow. And when clients begin to disclose more of themselves to you, you can follow them. To imagine what this is like, think of a game of tennis. One player serves the ball. The other does not wait for it to come to him, but goes to meet the ball and then either returns it to the server or plays it where the server has to make an effort to reach it. This analogy serves to illustrate a significant point about self-disclosing during counselling sessions. It is simply this. For the client and the counsellor to make progress they need to meet and know each other. Meeting and knowing each other makes explicit demands on both counsellor and client. If they are not simply going to meet but also to begin to know each other, they must be prepared to reveal information about themselves that they have never disclosed to each other before.

This takes courage on both sides. However, when clients and counsellors can share and care together they will have achieved one of the great milestones of practical counselling: open communication. Two examples might help to show you the difference between one-sided disclosure, the interrogative method, and two-way disclosure, the care and share method in practical counselling.

First consider a session where the counsellor is using one-sided disclosing.

COUNSELLOR: What is your problem?

CLIENT: My husband says I drink too much.

COUNSELLOR: How much do you drink?

CLIENT: I have never taken much notice, maybe three drinks.

COUNSELLOR: Per week, per day, per month?

CLIENT: Oh, about three per week.

COUNSELLOR: How large are these drinks?

CLIENT: What do you mean?

COUNSELLOR: I mean quantity and volume.

CLIENT: I don't think I am getting anywhere here. You sound just like my husband.

COUNSELLOR: I am not ...

CLIENT: Yes, you are.

COUNSELLOR: No, I definitely am not ...

CLIENT: Oh, but I'm afraid you most definitely are ... I won't be coming back here again ... *(Rises and leaves the room)*

COUNSELLOR *(to self)*: Typical, some people just don't want to be helped.

Now consider how this situation could have been so very different utilizing two-way disclosing.

COUNSELLOR: Good morning, Mary, this session is about discovering what you want to tell me about your situation as you see it. Where would you like to begin?

CLIENT: Well, my husband says I drink too much.

COUNSELLOR: Drink too much?

CLIENT: Yes, you know, he thinks I am an alcoholic and a hopeless wife and mother.

COUNSELLOR: You know your saying that reminds me of the time I used to get told off by my parents for doing things my sister did, and I used to get hurt and I resented it.

CLIENT: Exactly. I mean that is the way I feel about Kevin. He blames me for things, lots of things, and I get so nervous. It's always on my mind. Sometimes I get so mad at him ...

COUNSELLOR: So, Mary, you know what it is like to have strong feelings about Kevin and the things he says to you; this can occupy your thoughts so much you get nervous. Is that right?

CLIENT: Yes, I suppose that is how it is ...

COUNSELLOR: How sure are you? I mean, I remember how I used to worry a lot about what my parents said about me, because I wondered if they were right. Sometimes I was a bit unsure of myself.

CLIENT: No, it's not quite like that for me.

COUNSELLOR: I would be very interested to know just how it is for you, Mary.

CLIENT: OK, ahmm ... *(Hesitates for a long time, counsellor does not interrupt)* ... Well, I am going to tell you something I have never told anyone before … I don't quite know how to put it …

COUNSELLOR: Put it in any way that makes sense to you.

CLIENT: To me it's Kevin that should be sitting here, not me. I drink because he gets on at me so much and all the other things he blames me for … they only started when his younger brother died in a car accident.

COUNSELLOR: And he has blamed you since then …

CLIENT: Yes, it has just hit me just now what might be part of the problem between Kevin and me … *(Pauses and remains silent)*

COUNSELLOR: I know that feeling of being stunned into silence, I still get it when I have realized something important … *(Pause/silence)*

CLIENT: Yes … yes … I have just realized Kevin has been blaming me for Jim's death … I was the driver of the car …

Lessons to be Learned from Disclosing

These examples of one-way and two-way disclosing illustrate that there are many lessons to be learned from disclosing during counselling sessions. Perhaps the first is that it is unrealistic for counsellors to expect clients to make progress in counselling by simply closely questioning them. Careful questioning has been found to be one of the cornerstones of counselling, but, in my experience, this is best done within a climate of caring and mutual disclosure between the client and the counsellor. There will be times when the client asks questions of the counsellor and the counsellor of the client. Similarly, there will be many moments when there will be mutual and authentic sharing.

Another lesson we can learn from self-disclosure is its potential efficacy in enhancing the personal change process in clients. The counsellor should aim to use self-disclosing as a specific counselling skill and with the intention of influencing clients in the direction they are trying to move towards and the goals they are aiming to achieve. At best, self-disclosing can be employed by the counsellor as a powerful therapeutic ally that empowers clients to make significant changes in their lives, to consider new alternatives, to review their actions and to understand themselves better through the appreciation of other people's experiences. At worst, self-disclosing can produce mere trivia and can have no relevance to the clients' needs, the tasks they are trying to work at, or the problems they seek to overcome. At these times, self-disclosure can be a positive hindrance to desirable therapeutic outcomes in counselling.

One final point about self-disclosing. Research into counsellors who self-disclosed found that there seems to be an optimum climate created for self-disclosing, a bit like the fairy tale *Goldilocks and the Three Bears*. You remember Goldilocks tried three plates of porridge in the bears' house. One was too hot, one too cold, and one just right. Like all good fairy tales, it has a message beyond the literal. One message for counsellors is that too much self-disclosing is as unhelpful to clients as too little. The task for us is to get self-disclosing 'just right'. The just rightness of self-disclosing is to tailor our self-disclosing to the client, where they are, their stories, their concern and pain, and the options they might have for better running their lives.

Appropriate self-disclosure by the counsellor makes it possible for clients to tell their story, often for the first time. It is in the telling of their story that the seeds of change can begin to grow. And it is in embracing it, complementing it, enlarging on it, and utilizing what the clients say, feel and think, that the counsellor can make skilful contributions that create the conditions for client change.

Overview

●

In this chapter, we have seen there are a number of important lessons for counsellors who are serious about creating the conditions for change with clients who come for practical counselling. First of all, counsellors should convey to clients that they are trusted and respected for themselves and their views and their beliefs about their problems or personal difficulties. Trusting and showing respect for our clients is one of the essential ground rules of practical counselling. Along with this it is imperative that you create a climate of trust and respect in which clients realize they are being heard by the counsellor, and are hearing what their personal concerns mean to them. Clearly, it is not for the counsellor to select those portions of the client's experience and concerns that the counsellor thinks are important. On the contrary, one of the tasks of counselling is for counsellors to enable their clients to make sense of the reasons they are in counselling, what they need to get out of counselling, and what areas of their experience or personal difficulties they need to come to terms with or change. Hearing and being heard are achieved best with a clear emphasis on careful listening.

Careful listening means listening fully and with great care, showing interest and concern and empathy towards the client. Care is shown by being alert to the thoughts, feelings, beliefs, values and personal meanings that clients attach to their communications. By checking our understandings of clients and their personal worlds, counsellors can give timely feedback that not only confirms that we have understood the client but that lets clients know they have been understood. All of this needs to be carefully synchronized with the pace of counselling. We have seen how timing can be a powerful device in counselling and how it is essential not to go too slow or race ahead in counselling sessions when clients are not ready to do so.

Pacing the client needs to be coupled with appropriate self-disclosure by whoever is providing counselling. However, self-disclosure can facilitate or impede progress in practical counselling. It is one of the main responsibilities of counsellors to employ appropriate self-disclosure in a way that contributes to the changes clients see themselves as needing to make in their lives. Self-disclosure, therefore, should never be seen as an opportunity to chit-chat or gossip with clients. On the contrary, in the hands of sensitive, listening, and caring counsellors, appropriate self-disclosure empowers clients to understand their own needs and how they might better be satisfied.

Chapter 3

THE CLIENT-TASK FOCUS IN PRACTICAL COUNSELLING

Once we have created the conditions for change, what happens next? It is at this stage of practical counselling that some counsellors get mixed up, lost or simply are not sure how to continue influencing the counselling. Interestingly, research in human communication reveals that we tend to influence situations whether or not we say anything. Not saying something, or having a particular look on our faces, or the position we place our bodies in, all communicate. Silence, for instance, in practical counselling conveys its own message to clients and this can be perceived by them as helpful or as a sign that the counsellor is not interested in them or their difficulties.

Counsellors need to be clear about what it is they are trying to achieve in counselling sessions. In my experience with practical counselling I try to communicate three themes to clients. The first is that they are not alone but are individual and unique people in their own right. The second is that there is some task to perform. The third is that practical counselling is one way for people to discover the task or tasks they may need to undertake.

Attitudes and Needs

●

The client-task focus in practical counselling has three main dimensions to it: the attitude of the counsellor, the needs of the client, and the tasks to be undertaken in counselling. The counsellor aims for the right balance of being client-oriented or task-oriented at any one time in counselling sessions. The time dimension is a factor that some other approaches to counselling have ignored in the past. However, I regard time as an integral part of the counselling process, if only for the simple reason that counselling does not take place in a vacuum. The world does not stand still whilst the counsellor and client focus on their counselling sessions. The world outside the counselling room that is relevant to the client may change in between counselling sessions, or indeed as counselling is taking place. This is why it is essential that counsellors regularly review with their clients what has been happening since they last met and the kinds of tasks they want to address in counselling.

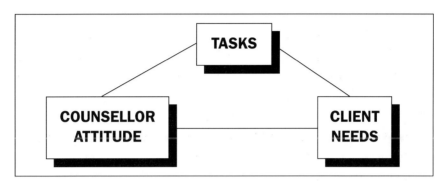

Achieving a good fit between the counsellor's attitude towards clients, the current needs of the client, and the tasks to be performed in or out of counselling sessions may not be easy. The counsellor does not always get it right. In some cases this may be a problem of getting the wrong emphasis, at the wrong time and in the wrong place. For example too much task orientation by the counsellor at the expense of communicating caring for the client can undermine previous progress in counselling. Being overly task-oriented, the counsellor may simply fail to reach any understanding of the person who has come for counselling. Clients can be quick to notice this and may object, confront the counsellor or refuse to continue. Unless this is part of the counsellor's intentions for the client, it makes for ineffective counselling.

There are exceptions to this situation, however. For instance, the counsellor may have understood the client to want to exercise a need to be angry or refuse requests by adults in the position of some authority over them. Clearly, counsellors should not run counselling sessions for their own benefit or satisfaction at the expense of their clients.

Another situation to avoid is where the counsellor and client meet for counselling sessions but end up having a nice cosy chat.

Being person-focused to the point where the counsellor and the client ignore the tasks they need to encounter may even amount to an implicit decision to do nothing. This does not imply that doing nothing is always to be avoided in practical counselling. Indeed, sometimes I find clients choose not to change their situation. Having reviewed where they are, the changes that they think they would like to make, and the effects they believe this would have on their lives, clients will in this process have gained some new and acceptable perspective on the situation.

It is the counsellor's role in practical counselling to influence the counselling process and to enable clients to focus on the choices that may be before them. It should not, however, be the counsellor's intention or purpose to make choices for their clients. In facilitating progress in practical counselling, the counsellor cultivates a combination of caring for the client along with a respect for their needs and the tasks to be faced.

Caring for Clients

I find that practical counselling works when I show that I care for clients and the clients know that I care for them. Counsellors who can show that they have developed a purposeful attitude of caring for their clients are in a position to help them change. Caring for clients does not mean approving of what they may have done or are doing in an attempt to overcome their personal difficulties. Caring for clients is no soft option. It can often be demanding work. For caring for clients should never be confused with the problems being experienced by the client. Clearly, the two are necessarily involved in counselling. However, counsellors deal with real people, not spare parts or machines. Counsellors who get results care for their clients and work with them on the problems or experiences that they would like to change. These counsellors have understood and adopted a central two-fold attitude essential for caring for clients. They are good at 'tough-loving'.

Tough-loving means prizing clients but not their problems. It involves genuinely accepting clients for what they are but wanting to empower them to be tough in finding the courage to face their problems. This is what counsellors are doing when they are actively prizing people. Prizing people for what they are despite their difficulties is what caring for clients means. Prizing them in their pain as well as their triumph says to the client, "I am with you." Sometimes clients improve simply because they perceive that you care about them and what they think and feel about themselves. On many occasions I have found clients are overwhelmed by emotions. Sometimes these emotions — anger, frustration, hurt, resentment and fear — have been held back for years by clients waiting for someone to care for them. The rush and release of these emotions are like a damburst of feeling that surges forward in the recognition and receiving of caring from the counsellor. During these emotional discharges, counsellors simply need to remind their clients that they are supported as well as cared for.

In these moments or episodes, it is best for counsellors to 'be available' to their clients, and for their clients to know they are accessible. Practical counselling proceeds better in these situations when the counsellor keeps in the background, and only comes to the foreground again to hold the client. Like J D Salinger's character, Holden Caulfield in *Catcher in the Rye*, the counsellor is there to catch clients and to support them through their experience of their emotions.

The counsellor's choice to move into the background or foreground should not be seen as an 'either/or' attitude towards the client. Rather it can be seen more like a child learning to walk. The child may need support for some of the time and at other times can take a few steps for itself, until it is quite capable of walking entirely on its own. The process is similar in practical counselling. You influence the process of emotional release by giving support where it is required, then beginning to withdraw it as clients take their own first steady steps towards the future, returning to support them again should they falter on the way.

Sometimes support can mean physical reassurance, at others just simple, soothing empathic support such as "It hurts", "You are feeling some things you have held back for some time", "It helps to let go after all this time" and so on. Other forms of support can be slightly more direct, such as "If he was here now what would you say to him?" or "Now you have that feeling where can you take it?" or "That cut-up feeling you have — who needs to be knowing about that?" and "Do what you feel needs to be done with those feelings now." On yet other occasions the counsellor simply respects the emotions and allows them to flow unhindered and interspersed with periods of attentive silence.

This is not the place to pursue specific counselling techniques as these are more thoroughly considered in later chapters of this book. However, these examples show the kind of supportive, facilitative progress that counsellors can make with their clients. The point for counsellors to grasp is, I hope, clear. Caring for clients embraces a specific set of attitudes. Caring for clients is accepting them for what they are at this particular place in life. It means tough-loving on the part of whoever is providing counselling. Caring for the client also means being supportive on some occasions and intervening in others. Above all, caring for clients is not some meaningless cliché that is bandied about by counsellors. Caring for clients is fundamental to therapeutic outcomes in counselling. Therefore, caring for clients puts a clear responsibility on our shoulders if we are engaging in practical counselling. It requires us to be alert to the needs of clients.

The Needs of Clients

●

Clients come to counselling mainly because they don't know how to satisfy their needs. This can either be as a result of not knowing what their needs are, or knowing what their needs are, but trying to satisfy them inappropriately. In practical counselling, counsellors concern themselves with recognizing the needs of clients; enabling clients to recognize their needs and how they are trying to satisfy them at present; and empowering clients to satisfy their needs in alternative ways, should they wish to do so.

Clients who come for practical counselling seem to have four sets of needs. When one or more of these client needs are not being met to a significant degree — or in an appropriate way — they experience personal problems. These four main needs are:

1   The need to feel safe and secure;
2   The need to give and receive affection;
3   The need to be included and to include others;
4   The need to control and be controlled.

Feeling Safe and Secure

Remember that when clients come to counselling they are taking a risk. They may have been referred by another caring professional, or referred themselves, or come as a result of somebody else recommending counselling. They may have come to counselling unwillingly or unsure of whether they want counselling or not. Therefore it is important that they feel safe and secure in coming to counselling if they are to continue with the sessions. A brief example shows how a counsellor helped a client to feel safe and secure in coming for a counselling session.

COUNSELLOR: Good morning, Sheila, please take a seat. I am glad you could come to see me. Maybe you could tell me how you came to make this appointment. Just tell me in your own way and in your own words ... *(Pause, nothing from Sheila, counsellor prompts)* Where would you like to begin?

SHEILA: I'm ... not really sure why I am here ... I am a bit worried about this, I mean I don't even know if I ... my problem ... er, my anxiety ... I ... came here because my friend thought ... it was a good idea ... *(Silence)*

COUNSELLOR: Sheila, I wonder how I could help you find out if you really want to be here. *(Counsellor uses similar language and formality; and offers opportunity to client to satisfy need to feel safe and secure.)*

SHEILA: Well, yes ... I ... would like that ... I mean, could I do that now?

COUNSELLOR: Do that now ... yes, of course. *(Counsellor reassures Sheila, repeats "do that now" and confirms it is OK, she is safe to ask.)*

SHEILA: Well, for a start I really want to know if you have helped other people with anxiety ... I mean, you have done this sort of thing before, haven't you?

COUNSELLOR: You're wondering if you would feel safe and secure enough if I was to work with you on your anxiety? *(Notice the counsellor puts the offer of counselling in the conditional tense and attempts to convey an understanding of Sheila's need to feel safe and secure. It's Sheila's anxiety, it belongs to her and the counsellor makes no attempt to take it away from her.)*

SHEILA: Yes, I suppose I am ... I mean, I don't feel quite so bad now.

COUNSELLOR: Now that ... *(Said with an inviting tone to carry on)*

SHEILA: I can start to tell you what is really bothering me.

Giving and Receiving Affection

Another fundamental human need is the desire to give and receive affection. Some clients try to satisfy their needs for giving and receiving affection in curious ways or ways that disable them or take away their dignity. The way they have learned to behave, think and feel to obtain affection or in their giving of affection can be heavily disguised. One of the characteristics of effective counselling is that clients are enabled to discover the ways in which they have been trying to satisfy their needs for giving and receiving affection, and to explore alternative options to satisfy these needs. Also counsellors can give affection and receive it during counselling sessions and this can act as a model for clients to work with on their own concerns, and the ways they are trying to satisfy their needs. Here is an excerpt from a counselling session with Malcolm, a 25-year-old unemployed man, referred for counselling with an alcohol problem.

COUNSELLOR: Malcolm, you say that there is nothing you can do about your drinking, yet you would like to give it up ... I would like it if you could help me understand this a bit more. *(Short summary, also counsellor shows interest in what Malcolm has to say.)*

MALCOLM: You wouldn't be interested ... it's nothing I can do anything about ...

COUNSELLOR: You may not be ready to tell me about it. But I am interested in what it is like for you ... But I don't want you to say any more unless you would like me to hear about it now.

MALCOLM: I had my first drink of alcohol when I was seven, just a kid. Ehm ... *(Coughs and clears throat)* ... It ... my problem goes back a long way ... I remember, I used to have to go to the pub and wait for my mum and dad to come out. They would be pissed and very friendly to me, gave me cuddles, kisses, presents, that sort of thing, you know ...?

COUNSELLOR: Mm ... cuddles and kisses ... yes, I know ... *(Counsellor maintains rapport and gives affection signals to Malcolm.)* So you went to the pub and got lots of affection from Mum and Dad when they had drunk a lot of alcohol?

MALCOLM: Sure, that's right.

COUNSELLOR: Right ... and I wonder what you might have experienced or learned from those times, Malcolm.

MALCOLM: Well ... I am beginning to see that when Mum and Dad were drunk I got a lot of loving from them ... and these times ... they let me show them how much I loved them ... I mean they let me do things for them ... I liked it then ... when we were all together ... Dad drunk and Mum falling all over the place. *(Counsellor allows Malcolm to tell his story.)*

COUNSELLOR: And when they were sober ... what was it like then? *(Focuses on what Malcolm hasn't mentioned, to bring it into his awareness)*

MALCOLM: Rotten. Dad bullied me and Mum would whip me round the legs with an old stick she kept in the cupboard. She used to say, "If you don't get out of the house you will get old whippy." So I had to keep clear of Mum and Dad when they were sober. They didn't like me when they were sober, or said they were needing a drink. I knew these were the signals that I might get a beating or it was time to be off and out of the house. It came to the point where I just used to try and see them when they were drunk. They were much nicer to me then and I could do things for them. They were great when they were like that.

COUNSELLOR: And when you look back at those times, what do they say to you now, Malcolm?

MALCOLM *(pauses, silence for a few moments between counsellor and Malcolm):* They say I might be drinking too much alcohol because ... that's the way I learned it from Mum and Dad.

COUNSELLOR: You learned something important from them.

MALCOLM: Yeh ... but I'm now feeling angry about it ... *(Realizes the needs he has been blocking or diverting)*

COUNSELLOR: Feeling angry about what you learned from them ... And that was ...

MALCOLM: The only way I could get their love or be loving to them was through drink and being drunk.

COUNSELLOR: What has happened since then, or don't you know?

MALCOLM: Oh, I know all right. It's hurting to talk about it now but I feel some kind of weight beginning to slide off my shoulders ... I can only give my gentler side to others when I am drunk, and let them in or give to me when I have had a good bout of boozing.

COUNSELLOR: Had you thought that there might be other ways you can share yourself with others and let them in? *(Counsellor begins to offer the opportunity to consider alternative ways to satisfy this need for giving and receiving affection.)*

MALCOLM: No, but I would seriously like to try something else. This way of life is hell.

COUNSELLOR: Malcolm, you have learned so much from your experiences with your parents and alcohol. You also know a lot about your own needs. Especially your need to give and receive affection. Let's look at some new ways you can satisfy these needs of yours ...

The Need to be Included and to Include Others

We all have the need for recognition and status. Early in our lives it shows when we respond to our names and feel good or bad about ourselves. When someone recognizes us it also confers status. It says you are important. You are included. When people who are important to us fail to recognize us we can feel hurt or rejected, angry or depressed. We feel excluded when our status is ignored and we do not feel important to ourselves or others. It affects individuals in different ways. Some people who come for counselling have yearned for years for recognition from particular people. They have an urgent, sometimes obsessive, desire to be included in what others do. They often have a low sense of self-esteem. They do not feel important or even useful. They believe they have a low status in the eyes of others. One of the first signs that a person is suffering from a lack of status, recognition and self-worth is becoming frustrated and angry. It all stems from the need to be included and to include significant others in our lives. When these needs are thwarted or remain unsatisfied people experience personal problems.

It certainly affected Dennis in this way.

DENNIS: Right, there is no way I am putting up with this, it's personal abuse ... She [Dennis's wife] thinks she can do what she likes, come and go without even talking to me about what she is doing ... I have had enough ... I'm leaving, leaving, I tell you, and then where will she be, eh, eh?

COUNSELLOR: You feel you're being ignored by your wife ...

DENNIS: Ignored ... you mean I don't exist for her ... and ...

COUNSELLOR: And that upsets you very much.

DENNIS: Yes, yes, too true I am upset. I am upset now ...

COUNSELLOR: You're upset now and you feel ignored.

DENNIS: Course I am ... what do I mean to her? She has all these friends ... out there. (Points out of the window)

COUNSELLOR: And where are you, Dennis?

DENNIS: I am here, feeling I don't matter to her any more. I don't count now ... if only ... if only ...

COUNSELLOR: You could ...

DENNIS: Get her to pay me more attention. That's it. I need her to tell me that I am still special to her ...

COUNSELLOR: Was there ever a time when you felt you were special to Kate? *(Counsellor checks to find out if things have been better in the past, and introduces the name of Dennis's wife.)*

DENNIS: Yes, oh yes, yes. *(Dennis's mood lifts to being cheerful as he recalls the past.)*

COUNSELLOR: I would like to hear about those times.

DENNIS: Well, Kate and I used to go fishing a lot, out on an old boat I had near the pier, and after the fishing trips we would go to the pub or a restaurant and meet some other people and have fun. We did that a lot then.

COUNSELLOR: So at the moment you don't particularly feel appreciated by Kate but there was a time in the past when you felt recognized and valued more by Kate than you do now?

DENNIS: Yes, that's right ... it was better then than it is now.

COUNSELLOR: Dennis, I want you to think very carefully about what it was you were doing then that made it possible for Kate to think you were so important to her. Can you do that for me?

DENNIS: Well ... let's see ... I used to take the trouble of asking her what she would like to do that day ... and then I would say what I wanted to do ... and I ... yes, it went like that and we decided together ... My God ... I have just realized something terrible, this moment ...

COUNSELLOR: I wonder what that is, Dennis.

DENNIS: Since we got married, I have tended to decide what we are doing without asking her. I suppose I just thought she would want to do what I did because I know her so well ...I thought I knew what she liked.

COUNSELLOR: I wonder what she might like most of all ...

DENNIS: After all this time it has occurred to me what's wrong. I stopped her making decisions. We stopped deciding and doing things. That is when I felt left out. That's when I started feeling unimportant to Kate. I suppose I did the same to her ...

The Need to Control and be Controlled

Anyone who drives a car knows what it is like both to control and be controlled by the vehicle and the traffic conditions on the road. If we want to arrive at a specific destination we choose our route and steer the car in the direction we want to go. However, along the road there are traffic lights and road works, and other vehicles going places. When traffic lights are red we stop. When there are road works we avoid them. When another car slows down in front of us, we slow down. Similarly, in practical counselling clients often show a mixture of wanting to control situations and also needing to be controlled under certain circumstances. The need for control and to be controlled can vary for each individual. It is the counsellor's responsibility to enable clients to know what they need to control or be controlled by, how much and in what ways.

Phyllis, a policewoman, showed how she needed to sort out her need for control along with the need to control others.

COUNSELLOR: Phyllis, you say that you just can't stand the thought of having the operation. Just how serious is this for you?

PHYLLIS: Well, the operation is quite minor. I have talked the matter over thoroughly with the surgeon and he seems to know what he is doing. He believes it will be over in an hour or so, but ...

COUNSELLOR: But you have some reservations about going ahead with it?

PHYLLIS: Not exactly reservations.

COUNSELLOR: How could you describe them so we can understand this better?

PHYLLIS: Well, ever since I can remember I have had to stand up for myself and help others. I grew up in a tough town and I saw so much unfairness and cruelty. That is one of the reasons I joined the police force.

COUNSELLOR: What specific reason was that, Phyllis?

PHYLLIS: To take charge of these people who take the law into their own hands, to help others, to take control of the situation.

COUNSELLOR: Taking control and helping others ... and your feelings about your operation are connected with this in some way, are they not?

PHYLLIS: Yes, they damn well are. It means giving control over to someone else. And a bit of me is saying that's what I want, but at the same time it means surrendering control.

COUNSELLOR: Phyllis, I want to ask you something. When something needs a police officer to help them take control of a situation, what do they do?

PHYLLIS: Oh, they either ring the station, put in an emergency call or just stop and ask me on the street.

COUNSELLOR: And they ask you to control the situation or support them in some way … Have I understood you correctly?

PHYLLIS: Yes, but it's not like that all of the time. Some people love it, at other times people don't like giving up control. They forget that you're a professional, trained for the job.

COUNSELLOR: And how do you see the surgeon? Is he a professional trained for the job?

PHYLLIS *(long pause)*:   Yes, I see what you mean …

COUNSELLOR: And when you put things into perspective …

PHYLLIS: Ahm, I see more clearly that I can feel confident in the operation and letting the surgeon take charge. I don't feel nearly as anxious about this little thing now …

A Word About Needs

A cautionary word is necessary about needs. First and foremost, if you are providing counselling you should be aware of your own needs in each session. Try not to confuse your needs such as feeling safe and secure with those of your clients. Counsellors may, and often do, benefit from the counselling sessions they offer their clients. However, remember, counselling is essentially for the client, not the counsellor. This does not mean to say that if you are a counsellor you should not benefit in some way from the counselling that takes place. There are times when counselling unintentionally has therapeutic effects for the counsellor.

Another practice to avoid is stereotyping your clients. Clients may have the same needs, yet these vary in degree. Indeed, the extent to which clients differ in their needs for feeling safe and secure, to give and receive affection, to include others and be included by them, and to control or be controlled, is what makes them individual. The counsellor's job is to understand the unique combination of needs for each person and it is the task of each person to come to know his or her own needs and the ways they are trying to satisfy them in their marital, domestic and occupational settings. This means being clear about why the client and counsellor meet for counselling sessions. They are there to pursue the tasks of practical counselling.

Tasks in Practical Counselling

●

Tasks run throughout practical counselling. They are central to the work of getting the job of counselling started, keeping it under way, and terminating the counselling contact. There are tasks for the counsellor and tasks for the client. These tasks govern the principles by which we formulate our ideas of counselling and the practices which we employ with clients. The tasks for counsellors and clients do not take on a linear perspective. That is to say we do not approach the tasks of practical counselling in an attitude of "First I do this, next I do this, which is followed by that." This is far too mechanical and probably explains why beginning counsellors often seem to be acting being a counsellor. To some extent this is something we cannot avoid in acquiring counselling attitudes and specific counselling skills. But what the counsellor can do is to adopt a number of guidelines which influence their practice and the tasks they pursue with their clients. The guidelines on page 61 show the different tasks for the client and the counsellor in practical counselling.

Clearly, there are many tasks that the client and counsellor engage in simultaneously or at different stages of their involvement during counselling sessions. There is no fixed formula for practical counselling. However, I have found these guidelines very useful for the counsellor and helpful for clients in practical counselling. Where counselling is effective you will often be able to see and hear yourself using these guidelines in your counselling sessions with clients. And you will be able to observe clients engaging in the counselling tasks that mirror those of your counselling efforts. These counselling tasks for the client and the counsellor also tend to form part of a larger change process in counselling, that is often characterized by change over time.

As counselling progresses so the tasks change for the counsellor and the client. For instance, when confidentiality and rapport

Guidelines for Tasks in Practical Counselling

COUNSELLOR TASKS	CLIENT TASKS
● Establishing confidentiality	■ Being satisfied with confidentiality
● Building trust and rapport	■ Reciprocating trust and rapport
● Accessing relevant information	■ Information searching
● Examining how client thinks/feels/behaves	■ Discovering own thinking/ feeling/behaving patterns
● Noticing what it important to the client	■ Understanding what is important to self
● Focusing on client's needs	■ Becoming aware of own needs
● Reviewing past/present/future ways of satisfying needs and if they are being met	■ Engaging/participating in reviewing with counsellor ways own needs have been/are being met
● Creating new choices with clients	■ Considering new choices with counsellor
● Challenging client's beliefs	■ Challenging own beliefs
● Utilizing client resources	■ Releasing personal resources
● Deciding desired outcomes and their implementation	■ Considering/deciding/pursuing desired outcomes
● Examining with clients how far needs are being met with new feeling/thinking/ behaving	■ Establishing new/feeling/thinking/ behaving to satisfy needs
● Pursuing and reviewing outcomes	■ Pursuing and reviewing outcomes
● Maintaining/breaking/ renewing client contact	■ Maintaining/breaking/renewing counsellor contact

are established the session becomes safer for the client and the counsellor to access and examine personal information, beliefs, and their thinking and feelings about any particular problem or concern. Conversely, progress in counselling can be significantly obstructed if the counsellor starts to try to delve into sensitive areas of their clients' lives without first establishing confidentiality and rapport. Without them, self-disclosure may never be possible. So the tasks of practical counselling need to be deeply respected by counsellors. This helps to set up a productive model of interaction between the counsellor and their clients, one which often facilitates change with clients. It may not always guarantee 'success' but, at minimum, I find following the tasks of counselling enables counsellors and clients to make progress in understanding the problems they are dealing with, their needs, and how they might better be satisfied.

Tasks: Present, Future, Past

The place of time and tasks is vital in practical counselling. They need to be present *and* future focused. The past does play a part. However, the main contribution it makes is to help the counsellor and client understand self-defeating ways that clients have used in the past to satisfy their needs and whether they are using them now in an attempt to solve their current problems. The focus of counselling is also to decide how far the particular ways clients try to satisfy their needs in the present lead to desirable or undesirable consequences for them in the future. The present focus in counselling sessions is upon finding out with the client what is happening now: "How is what you are doing now meeting your needs?"; "What is it like for you now?"; "As you are dealing with your situation in this way, what is occurring to you now?" These are all part of working with the client in the present.

The future focus is much more concerned with the counsellor examining with clients how the way they think, feel and behave now affects their future. "I am wondering how you think things will work out in the next few weeks if you carry on in this way"; "You seem to be saying you can foresee a time when this way of trying to satisfy your needs will turn into a disaster. Can you tell me who this is going to be a disaster for and specifically what you foresee happening if you don't change?" These are examples of how the counsellor influences the counselling process by focusing the client on particular tasks. In these examples we have emphasized the importance of how the counsellor would help clients understand the ways they have been trying to satisfy their needs and the consequences they or others may have to face should they wish to continue in this way.

Tasks in Context

Tasks take place in contexts and, wherever this is possible, appropriate contexts. The tasks pursued by counsellors and clients happen in shared and unshared contexts. Shared counselling essentially involves what goes on in each counselling session. Unshared counselling refers to what goes on outside formal counselling sessions. As many mature counsellors have observed, the real work of counselling often starts outside the counselling session. The counselling sessions plant and sow seeds and, if they fall on receptive ground, they blossom and grow outside in the real world of the person. Maybe they have a rocky start and then find a way of growing later on. Others just make a brief appearance and wither away.

Clients making changes in their lives or attempting to satisfy their needs in different ways go through a similar process. They try to succeed. Some try and falter. And sometimes they simply need enough courage to try to change by pursuing new tasks to satisfy their personal needs at the time. It is a matter of debate how directive the counsellor should be in deciding with clients the tasks they should pursue to make changes in themselves or others. I find this very much depends on the individual client. If, for example, you have a client who has been unable to satisfy his or her needs mainly because other people have made decisions for them throughout their lives, you need to ask yourself some searching questions and then check them with your client. For instance, where there is a theme of others making decisions for your client, does this person really need to have more control in his or her life and to begin making his or her own decisions for a change? Alternatively, where people like to be in control, yet want to be more included and welcomed into specific groups in or outside work, or want to be more cared for by their family, it may be more appropriate for the counsellor to work with them to become less controlling of others. Therefore, in practice, there will be times when it is appropriate for the counsellor to be quite indirect with clients and at others for the client to direct the tasks of counselling. However, over and above all of this it is the counsellor who must take responsibility for deciding the client tasks they will support, direct, agree to, or accommodate during counselling sessions. Clients have reciprocal responsibilities inside and outside counselling sessions. It is these mutual responsibilities for shared and unshared tasks that make up the tacit human contract between client and counsellor in counselling.

Tasks do not happen in a vacuum. Tasks are pursued and take place in contexts at home, at work and with friends and in families. It is therefore not only the job of the counsellor to work out with their clients the tasks they will take responsibility for, but also where they shall take place.

Counsellor Flexibility

●

In practical counselling, counsellors have to be very flexible in their approach to helping clients. As we have seen, practical counselling is guided by certain principles such as building trust and rapport, respecting the client, self-disclosing, gaining relevant information, utilizing the clients' resources and challenging them to consider new ways of satisfying their needs and finding the courage to put these into practice. Practical counselling is about staying with the tasks of counselling and keeping a client focus, so that clients can carry out their tasks in appropriate contexts, inside and outside counselling sessions. For all of this to really work and make a difference to people who come for counselling, counsellors have to be as flexible as possible in their practice.

In practical counselling, counsellors can and should be guided by clear principles, precepts and concepts and a model of the counselling process, but not bounded by theoretical dogma. Within this view of counselling, counsellors are then free to be much more flexible in the way they help their clients. The more flexible counsellors can be with their clients, whilst still maintaining a responsible and ethical approach to their work, the greater the potential opportunities for clients to solve or adapt to their problems and change the things they need to change in their lives. Conversely, the less flexible the counsellors and the narrower their assumptions about the client and how counselling should proceed, the fewer potential opportunities will be created for clients to benefit from the counselling they receive. The essence of the counsellor's approach in practical counselling is flexibility and knowing the model and concepts you are employing in counselling. Above all else, be flexible and be prepared to use a wide range of skills to empower your clients to benefit from counselling.

Chapter 4

A PRACTICAL MODEL FOR PRACTICAL COUNSELLING

Orientation to Using the Model of Practical Counselling

●

To use practical counselling effectively we need a practical model of counselling: a model that guides the counsellor and one which can be used in a flexible way during counselling. The RICOFR model (pronounced 'recover') for practical counselling allows us to do these things. RICOFR is an acronym for:

Rapport building
Information accessing
Creating choices
Personal **O**utcomes
Flexible **R**esourcing

The beauty of this model of counselling is its simplicity and its comprehensiveness and clear guidelines for counsellors. You can use it as a step-by-step process to begin with. Later, when you have more experience with the model, you can increase your ability to use whichever part of it you think is appropriate during counselling sessions. In the first instance, though, you should become familiar with the essentials of the practical counselling model and the way it can be used with clients.

Case Example • Rapport Building

Study this case example and notice how the counsellor is using the model of practical counselling to build rapport with the client.

COUNSELLOR *(sitting beside the client)*:   How can I help you today?

CLIENT: I don't know where to begin. *(Client is hesitant and apparently can't start talking; voice is quiet.)*

COUNSELLOR: It's difficult for you to know where you would like to start. I wonder what would help you to begin where it matters to you? *(Counsellor uses similar tone of voice, speaks quietly and at about the same speed as client and uses similar words, and ends with an invitation to begin where it matters most to the client.)*

CLIENT: It's Phillip.

COUNSELLOR: Phillip?

CLIENT: Yes, Phillip, my stepfather.

COUNSELLOR: You feel strongly about him . . .

CLIENT *(sounding much more animated and angry)*:   Yes, I do.

COUNSELLOR *(silence; waits for client to continue)*:

CLIENT: I suppose I feel so flat and worn out after all I have put into looking after Phillip. He is so demanding. I know I shouldn't feel this way but I really feel like a doormat. I just let him walk all over me.

COUNSELLOR: Phillip makes you feel this way.

CLIENT: Not just that. I have my own life to lead ... it's beginning to come to a parting of the ways for me and him ... I'd like to know how I can make the break.

Analysis

In this case the counsellor quickly developed rapport with the client. The counsellor used the language and tone of the client and avoided threatening the client by not sitting face on with her during their counselling session. The counsellor also spoke in the same rhythm and quietly like the client. The counsellor created good rapport whilst making it possible for the client to continue in the counselling session and to begin to speak more personally about herself and her concerns. The counsellor continued to sustain rapport and make it possible for the client to access and share important information about herself.

Practice

Next time you are with a client or in a training group observe how strong or weak your rapport is and how it is being achieved. Practice spotting the kinds of ways in which rapport can be strengthened and weakened in working with clients in counselling.

Case Example • Information Accessing

CLIENT: This anxiety is getting me down.

COUNSELLOR: How do you know it gets you down?

CLIENT: I feel my heart racing and my hands tremble – I sweat a lot at these times. Nobody seems to notice except me.

COUNSELLOR: Where do you notice it most?

CLIENT: Erm ... Oh, when I have to be near people, in trains, planes, buses ... and, yes, yes ... conferences or seminars where I have to be part of a small group ... so it's people ... I get this way when I am with people ...

COUNSELLOR: Are you getting it now?

CLIENT: Oh no ... I mean, this is different.

COUNSELLOR: I am wondering what you find specifically different about this situation.

CLIENT: It is different. It's just you and me isn't it ...

COUNSELLOR: That's right, just you and me. And what do you notice about you and me?

CLIENT: You listen to me and I ... er ... get on better with one person than a small group.

COUNSELLOR: OK ... so you are better with individuals than you are with small groups of people ...

CLIENT: Yes, that's right.

COUNSELLOR: In what specific situations are you better with individuals?

CLIENT: I am good at my job and I work with individuals there, especially when I'm doing appraisals with them.

COUNSELLOR: That is very interesting. You have excellent information about yourself. You know you feel anxious in small groups and you also know that you are better in face-to-face contacts with individuals, especially at work ...

CLIENT *(with growing interest and increased emphasis)*: True, very true.

COUNSELLOR: I'd like it if we could begin to understand what you are able to do that makes it better for you when you are with individuals. How does that feel for you?

CLIENT: I'd like to understand that as well ...

Analysis

In this case the counsellor did a number of things with the client, including asking for more information. The search for information was maintained with further sensitive questioning. At the same time the counsellor maintained rapport and respect for the client. The searching for information was backed up by checking by the counsellor and confirmation by the client. Also, the counsellor enabled the client to appreciate that he had personal resources to manage face-to-face interactions and thus implied that the client had abilities of his own. More information would be accessed so that the counsellor and the client would know the specific problem they were working with, whether the problem the client started with was the one he really wanted to work on or whether he could learn something from the skills he had for individual interactions that would be useful for him in his interactions in small groups of people. The sensitive counsellor may also have accessed information that the client did not want to have anything to do with small groups of people.

It is essential that counsellors spend sufficient time on empowering clients to access relevant information, feelings, thoughts and behaviours they have concerning their problems. It is important for counsellors not to jump to hasty conclusions in their work with clients. This is not to say they should not have hunches and speculations about their clients' problems and where they arise. However, these intuitions need to be tested with clients and confirmed or repudiated by them.

Practice

Next time you are with a client check that you are enabling him or her to access relevant information. Also make a point of asking yourself what information you might need to help the client and what information the client needs to help him or herself. One way of confirming that you have been able to access useful client information is being able to answer two key questions in practical counselling. First, do I or does the client have significant information that will help us understand this problem or situation? Second, have we managed to find abilities in the client or in the client's social network that could be utilized to overcome or manage these difficulties and personal concerns? Don't bulldoze ahead in getting this information. However, once information is made available that is relevant to your clients, you will have influenced the counselling process further. For once clients in practical counselling have information they can make new choices about how they think, feel and behave. Information gives clients choices.

Case Example • Creating Choices

CLIENT: I just don't know what to do.

COUNSELLOR: About what?

CLIENT: I mean now that I know how angry I am with my boss.

COUNSELLOR: You know you're angry with your boss?

CLIENT: Yes, it's his sexist manner — it really makes me boil.

COUNSELLOR: What is it he actually does that gets you so upset?

CLIENT: Oh, you know, always brushing past me, standing too close, making jokes about me ... my body ...

COUNSELLOR: If you had the choice how would you have him behave towards you?

CLIENT: Well for a start I would expect him to respect me and put a stop to all those awful lurid jokes and ... he would keep his hands off me ...

COUNSELLOR: So you would want him to be different to you in a number of ways, would you not?

CLIENT: I certainly would, if I had the choice. I feel so strongly about it all.

COUNSELLOR: Can you imagine for one moment how things would be different for you? Just suppose you are exercising these new choices. Really imagine it and tell me about it ...

CLIENT: It's much, much, better. I am in control. My boss doesn't take liberties. I'm not the subject of foul sexist jokes ... In fact I seem to be quite a changed person ... as I imagine it anyway ...

COUNSELLOR: And as you imagine it ... how are you feeling now?

CLIENT: My, my, I am surprised. I don't feel angry at all. In fact I'm feeling rather pleased with myself ... yes, a bit confident ... if you know what I mean ...

COUNSELLOR: This feeling ... the feeling of confidence you are experiencing now ... is that a good feeling to have?

CLIENT: Oh yes … I'd say it's a great feeling.

COUNSELLOR: How does it compare with that angry feeling you used to get?

CLIENT: I'd much rather have this confident feeling.

COUNSELLOR: You mean the feeling you're choosing to have now.

CLIENT: Yes, that's right, absolutely.

COUNSELLOR: OK, so you know the feeling you would choose to have and that is this confident feeling … and you'd like this feeling to continue with your boss …

CLIENT: Yes, I definitely would.

COUNSELLOR: Now you know that you can choose the feeling you want with your boss and that you can experience that feeling of confidence, I'd like to find out with you … the choices you can now make … about how you can take this feeling of confidence into your work and feel confident with your boss …

Analysis

The counsellor sustained rapport with the client and enabled her to access a number of pieces of information that were very significant for her. First, the client was having problems with a specific person — her boss. Second, she felt angry about the way he behaved towards her in specific contexts associated with work. Third, she wanted things to be different. Fourth, she knew when things would be different — she would have the feeling of confidence she was describing to the counsellor. The client did all of these things. With help from the counsellor, the client chose what information to access, which situations bothered her and with whom, the feelings she did not like and the ones she would rather have. On top of this the client was able to produce the feelings of confidence she would like to take into work. The counsellor influenced all of this by helping the client to choose the information she would work on and opening up opportunities for changing the way she feels at work with her boss. The counsellor influences the course of practical counselling. However, it is the clients who choose the information they need to work on and what they intend to do with it in the future. The counsellor's job is to actively create the conditions whereby clients can get access to information and choices that are important to them.

Practice

You will have gathered from this case example how critical it is for clients to make choices in practical counselling. Choosing information about how they feel, think, and behave in different situations and how much that needs changing is all up to the client. How much of your counselling sessions involves working with the client's information? Next time you see someone interviewed on TV or hear them on the radio, spend a little time deciding who is making the choices and what information is being used. Good interviewers use their information and make their choices. Often the unsuspecting people being interviewed never get their views across. However, those more accustomed to being interviewed make sure they convey their information and views and communicate their choices.

In practical counselling it is a responsibility of the counsellor to ensure that clients have the opportunity to exercise choice in the information they access and work with in counselling. Practical counselling is based on a client-driven agenda. The counsellor has a clear task. It is to empower clients so that they can have the best information that is available to them, and from this they can decide how they would like things to be in the future.

Case Example • Personal Outcomes

CLIENT: I am definitely prepared to try something different, anything to get some sleep at night. I haven't had a decent night's sleep in years.

COUNSELLOR: What have you tried already?

CLIENT: Oh, some sleeping pills and they worked but I still felt groggy all day and listless.

COUNSELLOR: How specifically would you prefer to feel when you wake up, and during the rest of the day?

CLIENT: Fresh and lots of energy — the way I used to feel.

COUNSELLOR: You know you would like to feel like you did before and that was more energetic and less lethargic. Recall for a moment how you used to feel ...

CLIENT: I can't see it. It's so much in the past, it's just a blur to me now.

COUNSELLOR: If you could clarify that blur what would it look like to you?

CLIENT: I can imagine myself being like one of those athletes in the marathon or the Olympics, stamina and keeping going, looking forward to the day as the sun rises each morning, ready to face the world.

COUNSELLOR: That's a great image. Stick with it and really know what you want from it for yourself and when you have found out and only then you can *let me know what you want* for yourself ... *(Emphasizes words "let me know what you want" and then pauses and is silent)*

CLIENT: I want energy.

COUNSELLOR: That's really good, you know you want energy and you know how you will feel when you have it. Is that right?

CLIENT: Nearly right.

COUNSELLOR: What is missing?

CLIENT: The initial effort — I don't even have the energy for that.

COUNSELLOR: You're absolutely right. You haven't enough energy to do something extra to ... make a start.

CLIENT: I'm well and truly stuck.

COUNSELLOR: You know the great thing about being stuck is you don't have to do more ...

CLIENT: What do you mean?

COUNSELLOR: You can do less instead of more to get that feeling of freshness and energy ... that feeling good in getting up in the morning and it's good to face the day.

CLIENT: I never thought of it like that before ...

COUNSELLOR: Think about it now.

CLIENT: Mmm ...

COUNSELLOR: You're thinking about it?

CLIENT: I'm thinking it's about time ... I asked my husband to share in looking after the kids and running the house ...

COUNSELLOR: Is that an outcome you would really like to experience ... and maybe do less instead of more of the same?

CLIENT: It's important to me. If I could it would mean getting to bed at a reasonable time and not having to wake up in the middle of the night worrying if the kids are OK and the laundry is done.

COUNSELLOR: It is important and you now have a clearer idea of what your outcome is for yourself.

CLIENT: I do.

COUNSELLOR: So what do you want?

CLIENT: I want to do less kid watching and less housework.

COUNSELLOR: Which one of these personal outcomes do you want to experience first?

CLIENT: Definitely less kid watching.

Analysis

The counsellor worked with this case on a number of levels. The first thing you might have noticed was the way in which the counsellor did not immediately accept that the outcome for the client was sleeping better at night. By applying information-accessing skills the counsellor discovered with the client two specific outcomes. One was for her husband to do more 'around the house'. The other was 'less kid watching'. We learn from this that one of the essential tasks for counsellors in practical counselling is to get access to the information upon which new choices can be made by the client. The second observation worth making is how the counsellor enabled the client to find out what new choices she had before her when she thought she was stuck. It is not uncommon in counselling generally for clients to confront counsellors with a general rut. Finally, the counsellor worked with the client to begin to be more specific about the personal outcomes she would like to experience first. The implication in this part of the counselling session is that the client has already started to work on her situation and the personal outcomes she would like to experience with her children and at home with her husband.

Practice

A lot went on in this counselling session. We have covered some of it in the analysis you have just read. Stop for a moment and consider these questions. What other things were going on that facilitated the counselling session? What kind of influence was the counsellor exerting? How was the counsellor doing it? How specifically did the counsellor enable the client to become clearer about her personal outcomes and what she wanted to experience in her life? What more needs to be done with this client? How would you ensure that this client was sufficiently committed to achieving the personal outcomes that she says are important to her? When you have done all of this, the next time you are counselling keep a mental note of how well your clients know what are their personal outcomes and how far these go towards satisfying their needs. It should prove to be very interesting and informative and add to your growing ability to use practical counselling with your clients.

Case Example • Flexible Resourcing

CLIENT: It's no good you telling me what to do to stop stealing. Everybody else has tried and I have always found a weakness in their suggestions and arguments. I'm a thief. Once a thief always a thief. I've been a thief ever since I can remember.

COUNSELLOR: That is very interesting. You don't want to stop being a thief. You enjoy being a thief?

CLIENT: No, you're wrong. You are like the others. But wrong in a different way.

COUNSELLOR: I'm wrong. I wonder how I am wrong in a different way from the others.

CLIENT: You really want to know?

COUNSELLOR: I really want to know, what makes me different from the others?

CLIENT: You are a bit spooky!

COUNSELLOR: Spooky?

CLIENT: Sure, you agree with me that I am a thief ... but I don't enjoy being a ... stealing.

COUNSELLOR: Let's see if we understand each other now. You and I agree you are a thief, but you don't enjoy being a thief and all the suggestions or advice you have had hasn't stopped you from stealing. Do we understand each other now?

CLIENT: Yeh, and anything you suggest I can find ways of criticizing it and show you why it won't work with me.

COUNSELLOR: That's great. I really need your help if we are going to do anything with this ... you are good at criticizing. I was just saying to someone this morning how there isn't enough criticism in working on problems . . . so many people take things for granted ... but I am not sure you are ready to solve this problem of yours. Maybe you aren't critical enough to do something about it.

CLIENT: I am ... I bet I'm more critical than you are.

COUNSELLOR: OK, are you critical enough to find a way of working on stealing? I mean really examine a way, put it into practice and give me proof ... I mean real proof that your way of giving up stealing is better than mine?

CLIENT: Easy ... and I can prove it too.

COUNSELLOR: Are you sure you are up to this ... it's not outside your abilities?

CLIENT: More up to it than you are.

COUNSELLOR: And I can feel free to criticize it?

CLIENT: Just try me ...

COUNSELLOR: What's your foolproof way of stopping stealing then?

CLIENT: Oh, I can do better than that ...

COUNSELLOR: How much better?

CLIENT: When I see you next time I won't have nicked anything and I'll have my stealing under control.

COUNSELLOR: Prove it and you'll prove me wrong ...

CLIENT: You are in for a big surprise ... a big surprise.

Analysis

In practical counselling the counsellor has to be alert at all times. You have to attend to the client, to every little detail. Why? Because all of the time we are sitting there wondering and thinking, "How can I help this person change and satisfy their needs more appropriately?" This means that counsellors have to be flexible in their approach. They have to be aware of the kinds of resources clients have that may be recruited to make change happen and achieve the outcomes they want for themselves. This case excerpt shows nicely how the counsellor was flexible and utilized the resources of the client in activating change. The first thing to notice is that the counsellor offered no resistance to the client. Second, the client's claims of being able to criticize and disprove all the efforts of previous therapists and counsellors were welcomed by the counsellor. Third, the counsellor utilized the client's abilities to criticize those who offered help to him and incorporated these into the client's efforts to solve his own problem of stealing. A fourth skill the counsellor brought into play was to use the position of the client and adopt it as his own. Thus the counsellor adopted the stance of doubting the client's abilities to solve his problem and inviting him to prove to the counsellor that he could overcome his stealing.

Practice

What did the counsellor do and not do that was useful in this counselling session? How do you approach clients and utilize their resources for personal change in their lives?

Take some time to think through the ways in which you can be more flexible in facilitating changes with clients in your counselling sessions. Choose a specific case you are working on now and help the client to introduce some new alternatives to manage or overcome his or her problems. Notice whether you are freewheeling and flexible with your clients or more systematic and rigorous in your counselling sessions. Which suits you best and which approach suits your clients? Review and evaluate your own counselling sessions with colleagues and if possible someone who periodically can provide you with appropriate supervision. Above all, strive to find how flexible you can be in helping your clients.

Overview
●

Practical counselling provides us with a practical model that can guide us when we are counselling clients. This guide provides us with a useful 'road map'. It reminds us that rapport needs to be established if counselling is to take place at all. It also suggests that for most purposes rapport should be sustained throughout counselling contact between counsellors and their clients. The model clearly points out that relevant client information is needed and it is on this information that clients can make choices about how they want to live their lives. Flexibility is the cornerstone of counselling contact with clients. During counselling, counsellors and clients are engaged in discovering new ways in which clients may satisfy their needs. The direction of practical counselling is towards enabling clients to know what outcomes they want to experience in their lives. The task of the counsellor is to empower clients to achieve their outcomes and live their lives more satisfyingly and responsibly.

Chapter 5

STARTING OFF

Preparation

●

How many times have you seen and heard a counselling session where the client has come for counselling and hesitatingly begun to tell the counsellor his or her story? It's a typical scene in counselling. The first counselling session is crucial for clients. They are often nervous, confused and uncertain. Nervous, because it is a new experience and they probably have many problems that have led them to come for counselling or be referred by someone else for counselling. Confused, because they need information to clarify their problems and how they might solve them. Uncertain, because they frequently do not know why they have come for counselling, and if they are doing the right thing in seeing a counsellor. It is therefore imperative that counsellors start off counselling sessions by enabling clients to feel good about coming for counselling or, at the very least, not to feel worse about having agreed to attend their first counselling session.

One clear purpose of the first meeting with clients is to congratulate them in many different ways for attending the counselling session. These forms of congratulating clients may also have to be repeated at later counselling sessions and in ways in which the clients can continue to feel motivated to work on their problems. Congratulating the client must be genuine. It should also be a subtle activity, but sometimes congratulating clients for attending counselling should be made explicit. Congratulating clients for starting their journey into counselling provides them with the message that they have made a 'good' decision. It does not ensure a trouble-free experience and counselling may indeed prove to be quite painful for some clients. Forgetting to congratulate the client for attending counselling is to lose an opportunity to start the process of counselling from the moment you make contact with the client.

Assignment

●

Let's look at these two case examples: one where the client was congratulated by the counsellor and another where the client was not. As you are reading them, try to imagine what it was like for the client; also what it is that the counsellor did or did not do that was crucial in the session. How did it affect the client? When you have done this write down how you would have handled the situation. You can do this part of the assignment on your own or with colleagues who provide counselling to clients.

Case Example One
Remembering to Congratulate the Client

COUNSELLOR: Good morning Peter, I am Veronica and I am your counsellor. I was expecting you. I am glad you could make it today.

CLIENT: Tell you the truth, it was my doctor who asked me to see you. I don't know why I am here …

COUNSELLOR: You can use being here to find out if you want to stay in this session and make future appointments.

CLIENT: I know I need to get over my mood swings — you know I tend to swing from being very kind of high and excited and then flip back into a black hole …

COUNSELLOR: I don't know if I can help you but I have worked with other people who used to have trouble with their mood swings.

CLIENT: You mean like mine?

COUNSELLOR: Now Peter, it would help if you could tell me more about these mood swings …

CLIENT: Well they seem to happen …

Analysis

In this case example the counsellor immediately makes the client comfortable. The counsellor introduces herself to Peter as Veronica and talks to him using his first name. She also expresses congratulation by saying she is glad that he could make it today. Two congratulatory messages. The tone is set as being welcoming but not jovial. At other points when Peter expresses doubt or uncertainty about coming for counselling Veronica answers his uncertainty by presenting the counselling session as a way Peter can be useful and use the session to make a decision about what it is that is bothering him and whether he would like to continue with future counselling sessions. As well as indirect congratulating, Veronica is saying to Peter: You made a decision to come here; if it is not what you want you can consider not coming for further counselling. Conversely, it makes it possible for Peter to know that, as well as being able to make a decision about his counselling, he also has the choice as to whether he will continue with his counselling sessions.

What other things do you notice were present or absent in this session? Now compare it with a session where the counsellor forgets to congratulate the client for coming for counselling.

Case Example Two
Forgetting to Congratulate the Client

COUNSELLOR: Good morning, please sit down. Now what can I do for you, Mr Tomkins?

CLIENT: I don't know ... er ... er ...

COUNSELLOR: Come on, Mr Tomkins, you must do better than that.

CLIENT: It is so difficult for me ... getting the words out ... I'm shy ...

COUNSELLOR: Look, Mr Tomkins, I run a very busy counselling clinic. Tell you what, I will just pop out for a coffee for five minutes ... give you time to think why you are here and what you want from my counselling sessions with you. *(Counsellor leaves the office.)*

CLIENT *(sits in silence staring at the floor):*

COUNSELLOR (*Returns to counselling room 15 minutes later to find empty room. Counsellor then walks over to receptionist in waiting room, saying in a loud voice)*: That Mr Tomkins has problems, doesn't he? Very silly man. *(Shouts down the hall)* Next.

Analysis

Notice anything different from the first case example? Make some mental notes of this or write them down in your personal notes. The counsellor did some awful things here. He did not make Mr Tomkins feel at ease. Immediately, the counsellor set the climate of counselling by being formal and distant, and made no effort to communicate to Mr Tomkins that he valued him for taking the trouble to come to his first counselling session. We don't know the counsellor's name and neither did Mr Tomkins. So who is Mr Tomkins going to relate to during counselling? How much of an obstruction is this for the counsellor, or for any progress that is to be made in counselling? And how is it affecting Mr Tomkins? These are all questions that need to be addressed in analysing this session. Preparing for congratulating the client is the first practical guideline to remember. When the client came for counselling, the counsellor did not welcome him, did not congratulate him, and did not make the first counselling session useful for him. The additional signals that the counsellor gave out all suggested he was too busy to see Mr Tomkins and, worse still, he was not really interested in Mr Tomkins. Only a few minutes into the session, the counsellor removes himself from the counselling room, essentially withdrawing any residue of rapport or support from Mr Tomkins. Is it then surprising that when the counsellor came back from his cup of coffee Mr Tomkins had left the counselling session?

The final insult to the client is when the counsellor announces to the crowded waiting room who he has been seeing and speaks of the client's problems. This counsellor has not only forgotten to congratulate the client. He has also conducted himself in a way that broke client confidentiality. What could the counsellor have done instead? How would you have tackled this problem? Think it over. See how you conduct yourself next time you are counselling someone who has come to counselling for the first time and is nervous, shy and confused. Observe yourself, or get someone to give you feedback on how well you did. How far did you remember to congratulate the client and what did this do for you, the client, the counselling session?

Summary

●

Congratulating the client is crucial in practical counselling. It provides clients with a clear indication that they have made a worthwhile decision. It also confirms that the client has the attention, concentration and respect of the counsellor. Congratulating the client is part of the counselling process and counsellors who ignore this do so at great risk to the client and to their own credibility during counselling sessions. Congratulating the client can be done directly or indirectly, subtly or obviously. It is part of the activity of attending to the client and building rapport. Congratulating clients is a way of saying to them that they matter and what they have to say, what they feel, what they think counts and is valued by the counsellor. Forgetting to engage in congratulating the client can at best hold up and inhibit the progress that can be made during counselling sessions. At worst it can create a climate between the client and the counsellor that destroys the hope of any working alliance. When this happens counselling contact may be terminated by the client. Clearly, congratulating is a counselling skill that counsellors should not forget to practise with their clients.

Chapter 6

OPENING & CONTINUING

Preparation

●

The start of a practical counselling session can do three things. First, it tends to set the scene for how the rest of the counselling session is conducted. Second, it makes it possible for the counsellor and client to continue to work together and make progress in counselling. However, a third possibility is that the way counsellors conduct themselves can actually inhibit the progress of counselling and limit the client unnecessarily. In their work together, an implicit contract is in evidence from the moment the counsellor has contact with the client. Sometimes this scene setting or climate creating gets off to a bumpy or unsatisfactory start and then rapport is established and counselling proceeds in earnest. At other times counsellors do not seem to have any real difficulty in talking with clients, and clients begin quite rapidly to explore their concerns, hopes, fears and interests.

What is it that makes the difference between counsellors who make progress with clients and those who seem to get stuck very early in their counselling sessions with clients? In the first instance, the counsellor who makes progress with clients knows how to use opening and continuing skills. The counsellor who gets stuck is at a loss as to how to use appropriate opening and continuing skills. One counsellor knows what to say after first greeting clients, the other does not.

Opening and continuing skills in practical counselling are those specific verbal counselling skills that make it possible for clients to begin counselling and continue to become involved in exploring their problems and experiences of what is significant for them. These verbal skills entail a sub-set of skills. These include:

1   The words used;
2   The order of the words;
3   The tonal quality of what is said;

4 The timing of what is said;

5 The context in which they are said.

Case Example
The Problem of Silence in Initial
Counselling Sessions

CLIENT *(client enters room)*:

COUNSELLOR: Good morning, Mrs Forbes.

CLIENT: Good morning,

COUNSELLOR: Please sit down.

CLIENT *(client sits down)*:

COUNSELLOR *(sits in silence for 20 minutes)*:

CLIENT *(sits in silence for 20 minutes)*:

COUNSELLOR: I'm afraid we have to stop there, Mrs Forbes.

Analysis

This example shows one of the least productive aspects of approaching practical counselling by simply waiting for the client to start talking. First of all, clients often wait for the counsellor to lead them. At the very least, the counsellor has the responsibility to provide a context for conversation, and this is better done by asking appropriate questions. A second problem in this case is the way the counsellor sets the scene for future counselling sessions. The first session can set the themes for future meetings between counsellors and their clients. All that clients like Mrs Forbes have to go on from their counselling sessions is that they learn to sit in silence, start talking, or stop attending counselling sessions. Silence in counselling sessions can be very effective in helping clients. However, introducing the client to practical counselling with a wall of silence is frequently unproductive and can actually impede and obstruct client progress.

Case Example
Appropriate Use of Opening and
Continuing Skills

COUNSELLOR: Good morning, Mrs Forbes, my name is Stuart. Please sit down; would you prefer the chair by the window or this one next to me?

CLIENT: I'd like to sit by the window, thanks. *(Sits down and is silent)*

COUNSELLOR: What name do you like being called by and would that be the one I can call you by?

CLIENT: Er ... I am ... I like to be called Judy ... you can call me Judy.

COUNSELLOR: Thanks, Judy ... Now would you care to tell me why you have come to see me.

CLIENT *(pauses)*: That's difficult for me ... I've never done that before ... I thought you would tell me why I am here . . . I have seen so many experts ... it's all in my file ... You're the first that wanted to know my name. I mean my favourite name — Judy.

COUNSELLOR: Now, that is very interesting, Judy. I would like it if you ... take your time, we don't have to be in a hurry. Just tell me in your own words what is bothering you ... You have been referred to me by your doctor ... but it is your story I am interested in. You can help me a lot by putting me in the picture ... would you like to start?

CLIENT: My guilt.

COUNSELLOR: Your guilt?

CLIENT: Yes, I feel it more and more these days. It's beginning to cripple me.

COUNSELLOR: How long have you felt this way?

CLIENT: Oh, about three years now.

COUNSELLOR: Three years ... please go on.

CLIENT: My first memory if I go back is just under three years ago. I got divorced and left my two kids Billy and Sonia with my ex-husband. I feel really awful thinking about that. It bothers me a lot ... I can't sleep at nights any more ... this guilt, it runs right through me now ...

Analysis

In this case example, the counsellor uses appropriate opening and continuing skills. Which specific ones did you notice? There were quite a few. Initially, the counsellor welcomed the client. The counsellor also immediately established where the client wanted to sit and by what name she wished to be called. Following this, the counsellor used selected words from the client and the client eventually started to tell her story to the counsellor. You can notice how, compared to the previous case example, the counsellor never left it entirely up to the client whether or not she would start talking. There is a lot going on in this case example. For instance, look at the way the counsellor keeps using the word 'now' and how the client eventually uses the word 'now'. 'Now' serves the purposes of focusing the counselling session in the present and permitting the client to continue to tell her story. The tonality of the counsellor is empathic but never condescending and the order of words used makes it possible to open up the problem that the client wishes to talk about. The counsellor has also implicitly set the context for counselling sessions that may follow. Refer back to the sub-set of skills for opening and continuing counselling sessions with clients and you will find that many of them were evident in this case.

Assignment

●

Get together with some colleagues and discuss the uses of appropriate and inappropriate opening and continuing skills in practical counselling.

Now specify those opening and continuing skills you find helpful and that you will practise with your clients.

Practise using those opening and continuing skills. Do this for 10 minutes each.

Break up into groups of two. Take turns in being client and counsellor. When you are the counsellor use as many opening and continuing skills as you think are appropriate for working with the client.

At the end of each practice session ask the person who plays the client to give you feedback on your opening and continuing skills.

Pursue your own questions and come to your own decisions about opening and continuing skills.

To get started you may find it useful to consider such issues as:

1 How appropriate was the counsellor's use of opening/continuing skills?

2 What specifically did the counsellor do that inhibited/impeded the client?

3 What kinds of phrases or words, and in which order, did the counsellor use and how did they help or hinder the client?

4 How far did the tonality of the counsellor fit with making it possible for the client to tell his or her story?

5 Where was the counsellor obviously using opening and continuing skills and where was the counsellor seeming just to have a conversation with the client? Which seemed to help the client best and why?

Make a note of what you have learned about your opening and continuing skills and how you can best use them with clients during counselling sessions. (See *A Practical Guide to Opening and Continuing Skills*, page 89.)

Summary

●

Opening and continuing skills are fundamental to practical counselling. Being able to acquire and develop the skills for opening and continuing counselling sessions with clients is a necessary goal for all counsellors. The degree to which opening and continuing skills are used appropriately in counselling can impede or enable clients to tell their story and voice their concerns.

There is a sub-set of skills involved in opening and continuing that can be used effectively in counselling sessions. These involve the words used by the counsellor, the order in which they are used, the tonal quality with which they are spoken, the timing and point at which they are used, and the context in which they are expressed. Opening and continuing skills should be practised until they become natural and are easily and appropriately utilized by counsellors for the benefit of their clients.

A Practical Guide to Opening and Continuing Skills

Keep practising your opening and continuing skills until they come naturally to you and clients feel comfortable working with you. Use this brief practical guide as an aid to acquiring your own range of opening and continuing skills that you can use with your clients.

OPENING SKILLS

- "Hello, I am . . ." (name)

- "Glad you could come today . . ."

- "Can you tell me how you feel about . . .?"

- "You have been referred to me by . . . for . . . Is this how you see the problem?"

- "Where do you think you should start?"

- "Would you give me an idea of why you wanted to see me?"

- "Please sit down . . . now, tell me what is on your mind."

- "How do you see your situation?"

- "Where would you like to begin?"

- "How are you today?"

- "What seems to be the difficulty?"

- "How have things been working out since we last met?"

- "Tell me where/what you need to work on today/now."

CONTINUING SKILLS

- "I see . . ."

- "Yes, please go on . . ."

- "Carry on . . . I'd like to hear your version of events . . ."

- "Uh, uh . . .mm . . . mm . . . aha . . ."

- "That is interesting . . . what happened next? . . . tell me more about . . . and then you/he/she/they . . .?"

- "I am with you . . . so you . . ." (repeat key phrase used by client)

- "And what feelings did this bring to you next?"

- "I can imagine."

- "And when you . . . I wonder what that felt like for you/her/him/them . . ."

Chapter 7

MATCHING & MIRRORING FOR RAPPORT

Preparation

•

Rapport is essential in practical counselling. Rapport provides the bridge between the client and the counsellor. The bridge allows the counsellor and the client to meet each other at different points on the bridge. Anyone who has built a bridge, scaled down or full-sized, real or imagined, knows what a bridge does. It brings two things together that could not meet otherwise. Sometimes the counsellor will cross the bridge to meet the client. At other times, clients may venture onto the bridge to share aspects of their lives that they have never shared with anyone else before.

These sharings provide the content of material and information that the clients wish to work with and use to examine how well they are satisfying their personal needs. Now the important point about these sharings is this. They don't just happen by accident or mistake, by chance or by error. They happen because the counsellor creates the conditions where clients can start sharing their personal information. The counsellor makes it possible for clients to ask themselves how they are trying to satisfy their personal needs and whether they need to change themselves or their situation. In doing so, the counsellor has to build rapport that is solid and lasting; that reaches out and meets the client; that builds a bridge between the world of the counsellor and the world of the client. Counsellors have to be good at building bridges.

First of all they need to know that a bridge has to be built between themselves and their clients. They know that without the bridge little productive counselling can take place. Second, and equally important, they need to have available to them all the skills of the master bridgebuilder. Counsellors need to be skilful at building rapport. Rapport-building skills come easily to competent counsellors. Third, they need to be able to build rapport with all kinds of people who come for counselling: agreeable clients and disagreeable clients; co-operative clients and unco-operative clients; submissive and aggressive clients; pliant, uncompliant and compliant clients. The list is endless. However, in practical counselling, the counsellor is expected to be able to build rapport with every client. Fortunately, we know a great deal about the skills required for building rapport with different clients. These skills are known as mirroring and matching.

Mirroring and Matching

•

During counselling sessions, counsellors carry out mirroring and matching with their clients. Mirroring involves counsellors producing exactly the behaviours of clients at particular periods during counselling. Matching is similar to mirroring, except matching is about making close approximations to the behaviours of clients. Matching and mirroring have a great deal in common, but are not the same. Mirroring involves producing a mirror image of the client. You can understand this for yourself. Stand in front of a mirror in your own home and notice how you see yourself. But it is a reflected and reversed image, a mirror image. If you lift your arm, shake your head or nod it, smile or frown, move different parts of your body, they are all mirror images of your self. If you wanted to match you would not be able to do that with the mirror. For instance, instead of producing an exact copy of a client's breathing you could match the rhythm of their breathing, and the rise and fall of their chest, with similar rhythmical movements, perhaps the rising and falling of one of your hands. There are many, many ways to carry out mirroring and matching with clients. You can use them to build rapport and break rapport. You can use them to be with the client and lead the client during counselling sessions. One of the main points to remember about building rapport with mirroring and matching is to link it to the needs of the client. A client who comes to counselling and is agitated, anxious, manic or angry needs to be met with appropriate mirroring and matching. The same principle is applicable to any client. It is going to be difficult to achieve good solid rapport if the counsellor adopts the same attitude and behaviours towards every client. Remember in practical counselling we have to be flexible in meeting the needs of clients.

Matching and mirroring requires tailoring to each client. Counsellors acquiring the skills of matching and mirroring usually discover how rapidly they can establish and retain rapport with their clients. They also appreciate a number of other things about matching and mirroring. They find that:

1 Matching and mirroring are not crude movements or behaviours;
2 Matching and mirroring are not obvious to clients;
3 Matching and mirroring are not the same things;
4 Matching and mirroring achieve rapid rapport with clients;
5 Matching and mirroring skills are quickly learned;
6 Matching and mirroring can be used with any client.

Just how effective matching and mirroring is with clients depends on how flexible the counsellor is in utilizing opportunities for building rapport. Different degrees of rapport can be seen in the everyday activities of people. The handshake is one of the most fundamental forms of matching and mirroring. It signifies some indicator of minimal rapport. Clearly, when someone does not wish to shake our hand or return a handshake, then there can be good reason to infer that we have trouble with rapport. People shaking hands after an argument or kissing and making up is a way of saying they have got some harmony back in their relationship. They are prepared to mirror and match again. Asking them to do this in the middle of a blazing row would be doomed to failure. So mirroring and matching also has to be timed very carefully in our work with clients. Timing your use of matching and mirroring in building rapport is crucial.

Case Examples

Look at these two case examples and keep the following questions in your mind. Which counsellor achieved satisfactory rapport with the client? How was it done? What prevented the counsellor establishing rapport in the other case? How could it have been improved?

1 • Susan

COUNSELLOR: Come in and sit down over there *(Points finger to small wooden chair in darkened corner of the room, turns back on Susan then sits on plush chair, faces the window and stares out into space. He does this throughout most of the counselling session.)*

SUSAN *(comes into room and sits down and speaks in whispers)*: My mother sent me ... she thinks ... says ... I need help.

COUNSELLOR *(sitting opposite end of room behind desk and talking to Susan in a loud, booming voice)*:   Right, Susan, let's hear all about it ... and I don't want any excuses. Your mother knows best. Right, carry on. Well, go on Susan.

SUSAN *(still speaking in a whisper, only even quieter now and pausing for a minute or so between her words interspersed with sighs)*:   Erm ... Mother ... she ... says ... I should eat ... more.

COUNSELLOR: Damn right. Look at you, Susan. I mean, have you seen yourself recently? Just skin and bone ... You need three square meals a day ... lots of steak. Isn't that right, Susan? Susan, I said steak. Are you listening to what I am saying? I agree with your mother.

SUSAN: I'm sorry, I mean .... it's not what my mother says ... anyway I am a vegetarian ... I don't think you ... erm ... understand. Can I go now?

COUNSELLOR: No, not yet, Susan, not by a long shot. Not until I have got to the root of your problem.

2 • Barry

COUNSELLOR: Barry, thanks for coming, please sit where you want to. *(Counsellor notices Barry is agitated and restless so welcomes him in a restless manner, briskly welcoming him and moving similarly to him and matching some of his hand movements. Barry quickly sits in chair and then counsellor makes a few quick gestures and sits abruptly as well.)* Now Barry, what seems to be concerning you today?

BARRY: I am going to blow at any time now … I feel it … I am ready to go round there and … and … take what is rightfully mine. *(Said with a mixture of anger and hurt in his voice)*

COUNSELLOR: Feel it Barry, it's about time you found a way of getting what is rightfully yours … you can find ways of going round. Now, how about it? Tell me what is rightfully yours. How are you going to get it? *(Said with same tonality and force of mixed anger–hurt feeling as Barry and a hint of a similar accent, and at the same time making a foot movement that matches Barry's breathing, only the foot movements are just that little bit slower in tempo to the breathing, sitting position mirrors Barry's posture)*

BARRY: Yeh … well it's about time I calmed down and started to just take some steps to get my job back … I was unfairly dismissed from work … and now, well, there's the mortgage … the kids. My wife is at her wits' end … and that damn manager, the one that lied … about me being drunk at work … *(Now less agitated, breathing more relaxed, more rational but yet has strong feelings about losing his job, he thinks unfairly)*

COUNSELLOR: And as you can calm down, you can start moving towards taking some action to get back what you think is yours. *(Said in a much more measured manner, agreeing with the idea of Barry getting back something he has lost, but not saying exactly what that is or how he should go about what he does next)*

BARRY: That's right … I feel more ready to do that now. You seem to know what I am going through.

COUNSELLOR: That's right …

Analysis

In Case One, the counsellor failed to mirror or match a vast number of behaviours exhibited by the client. In fact a great deal of misting (failing to mirror) and mismatching was occurring between the counsellor and client. All of this misting and mismatching resulted in lack of rapport. The client felt the counsellor did not understand her. The counsellor assumed he knew about the client and her problems. Indeed the counsellor made a fundamental error. He assumed Susan had a problem, rather than using matching and mirroring as ways of building rapport to check with Susan what she thought the difficulty was that she was experiencing. After all, it could have been her mother that was the problem, could it not? Other signs of mismatching were evident in the pace and tone of the counsellor's voice, the body posture, and the way right from the start of contact with Susan that the counsellor gazed out of the window when he was attempting to talk with her. These and other small and subtle signs, such as pointing and failing to notice the quality of voice in which the client was speaking and how diffident she was, all made rapport impossible with Susan. It is, therefore, not surprising that her discomfort was increased by the counsellor and she wanted to leave the counselling session as soon as possible. However, even this choice was taken away from her through the attitude of the counsellor. This last point is important. Why? Because matching and mirroring are skills and can be easily learned. However, they are at their most potent in practical counselling when they are integrated with other skills such as listening and become part of the counsellor's attitude towards counselling clients.

Case Two gives some idea of how matching and mirroring significantly contribute to building and strengthening rapport with clients. The counsellor very quickly started to match and mirror the client's behaviours. In particular, the counsellor used a similar tone of voice and accent and mirrored Barry's body movements and posture. From time to time the counsellor made rapid movements and then began to slow these movements down and make them more co-ordinated. In this case rapport was built quickly by following Barry. But it was also strengthened by the counsellor using some key phrases used by Barry, and meeting Barry's feelings of anger and hurt with similar ones. The counsellor went further and began to influence the counselling session by introducing calmness and readiness so Barry could begin to consider his position in a more rational way. Matching and mirroring can be carried out by the counsellor at several different levels. In the first case this was absent. In the second case, the counsellor matched and mirrored postures, movements, voice quality, tone and accent and emphasized some key phrases and words used by the client.

Assignment

•

This assignment has two parts: the first is observational and the second is experiential.

Observational

Look around you and see the stream of people in situations with other people. People in offices, in clubs and pubs, people at home and people you come in contact with daily, on your way to work, or on your way home. How much rapport have they got? Which pairs or groups have a deep rapport and which do not?

What is the difference in rapport between two lovers and two strangers meeting for the first time? What specific matching and mirroring skills do they use or not use that help to develop rapport or make rapport difficult to achieve?

You can make mental notes of this or keep a written record. Whichever method you adopt, it should help you acquire the matching and mirroring skills you can use to build and retain rapport with clients.

Experiential

Meet a friend or partner and notice the level of rapport you share with them. What are the matching and mirroring skills you are using? Which are they using? How easy is it to use them with this person? What is most difficult? What needs improving? How will you do it? Next, meet someone who you don't know. This can either be someone that shares a train journey to work or some other stranger at work or in your personal life. First check the level of rapport between you and then start to match and mirror their behaviour and notice what happens. Remember to mirror postures and gestures exactly and in matching use similar behaviours but not the same as those you observe. Also, listen for the opinions of the other person and agree with these and expand on them in some way. Finally, use a similar voice pattern and tonality and pace and use some of the phrases, words and ideas used by the stranger. Now gauge your level of rapport with them. How much of an improvement was there? What happened?

Summary

●

Establishing and retaining rapport is necessary for all practical counselling. It provides the bridge between the counsellor and client that allows counsellors to examine the needs of clients. It also creates the conditions where clients can lay the foundation for exploring their problems and potential solutions. Rapport is achieved through matching and mirroring skills. Mirroring involves accurately producing the behaviours and mannerisms of clients. Matching is used to copy client behaviours but not in order to mimic exactly what they do. Rather, matching takes the essential elements of the client's current activity but feeds them back to the client in less direct ways. Mirroring is more direct. Matching and mirroring are used by counsellors to build rapport with any client. Therefore counsellors need to be flexible in the way they utilize the behaviours of their clients for building rapport during counselling. Rapport needs to be created for counselling to begin, and to continue. Counsellors should aim to use a wide range of matching and mirroring skills. These may involve matching and mirroring posture, movements of the hands, arms, face and legs. Matching and mirroring extend to the tone of voice used, pacing of the voice and the use of clients' accents and the ideas they bring to counselling. Counsellors can quickly learn the skills of matching and mirroring and integrate these with their other counselling abilities.

Chapter 8

OBSERVING & LISTENING WITH UNDERSTANDING

Preparation

•

Observing

Counsellors notice things. Great counsellors are good observers. They notice the significant behaviours, mannerisms, thoughts, feelings and actions of their clients. They notice the way their clients dress, talk and walk. They notice the tone of their speech and the words they use. They pay attention to the obvious and the not so obvious. They see and hear what the client presents on the surface and they perceive the needs of their clients, those that are being satisfied and those that are not. They attend to the deeper unsatisfied needs of clients and those which they are attempting to satisfy through inappropriate ways. Observing is an essential skill in practical counselling. Observing needs to be consciously practised. There are two reasons why. These are best explained by a simple story.

Once, in the National Portrait Gallery in London, a visitor was viewing a self-portrait of Lucian Freud and comparing this to a photograph in a newspaper. After some time looking at the portrait, the visitor was heard to remark that the portrait did not look a bit like Freud. However, from the artist's perspective, the portrait spoke more truth about himself than any photograph. The first point about the story is that simply looking at someone is not enough. We can look without observing anything of significance about people. It is all the more important with clients who come for counselling. Counsellors go beyond looking when they start observing their clients and what matters to them. The second point is this. When we know what we are looking for, we can suddenly find we become better observers. Next time you are with a client or colleague start to notice things about them you overlooked before. The chances are you will begin to notice things about them that were there all of the time 'right in front of your eyes'.

Observing is fundamental to practical counselling. There is the dynamics of observing and the structure of observing. The dynamics of observing involves the counsellor in finding out valid answers to the question: What is going on with this person? These observations may depend on the external presentations of clients, the 'what you see is what there is' level of observing. There is also what is going on internally within clients. Here we have the phenomenon where a client's internal state, mood, thoughts, emotions and feelings are not directly observable. Yet it will often be through reasonable inference based on what the counsellor observes in the surface expressions of the client that valid observations can be made about clients and their concerns. It is also important to check these for our understanding of the client.

Observations need careful handling and nurturing. Counsellors who are proficient at observing are like artists, they see the meanings of what they are looking at. However, counsellors are like scientists as well. The observations we make of clients and about clients have a structure. The counsellor observing as artist is concerned with the meaning of what is happening. The counsellor as scientist is concerned with discovering the facts and the structure of their observations. Here, counsellors need to observe what, where, how, when and which specific patterns emerge from their observations of clients in counselling. On this basis, when the art and science of observing are practised by counsellors the deeper picture of the client emerges.

The deeper picture is not a static profile. It is more like a movie. In observing clients, counsellors should keep in mind that their clients are not stereotypes and may be the same or different in different situations with different people.

Observing clients is a prerequisite to understanding them, why they are in counselling, and what they hope to get out of their counselling sessions. In order to do this productively, counsellors can develop their listening abilities to improve their understanding of their clients.

Listening with Understanding

If there is one thing counsellors need to be competent in, it is listening to their clients. Without listening there is little understanding of clients or their personal difficulties. Listening with understanding is a set of skills rather than one specific skill. Listening is also an attitude that the counsellor should attempt to develop and continuously work on. In saying this we need to know when we are listening with understanding and when we are not.

What are the key elements of listening with understanding? The first requirement is that counsellors really have to know when they are listening to their client, and cultivate listening to their clients and understanding what they say. Listening is an active process. It requires the counsellor to deliberately attend to what clients are saying. This is crucial to practical counselling. There are two sides to listening with understanding. First, counsellors need to know they are listening to and understanding their clients. Second, and of equal importance, clients need to know they are being listened to and understood. The two are essential to practical counselling.

Listening with understanding for the counsellor means being able to work with clients so they can both discover if the clients are satisfying their needs or if they want to change the way they are attempting to satisfy their needs. In practice, for the counsellor, this means listening to learn, and learning to listen.

In listening to learn, and learning to listen, what is it that counsellors can learn that will be of help to their clients? Listening to learn means being able to learn from clients. It is the clients who help the counsellor understand their problems. The counsellor's task is to listen in a way that helps them understand their clients. The first guideline therefore in listening with understanding is learning to listen. To do this one must be clear about those skills and attitudes that facilitate listening and those that block listening with understanding.

Study the guide to *Listening with Understanding* (page 102) and become familiar with those skills and attitudes that facilitate or block counsellor contact with clients. Which is more typical of you, your colleagues, other counsellors you know? In your own counselling sessions are you inclined to be facilitating or blocking when you are engaged in observing and intent on listening with understanding? Which specific clients, male or female, do you find you are listening to with understanding and facilitating more than blocking during counselling? Why?

How will you continue to improve your ability to listen with understanding?

Case Examples

Clearly observing and listening techniques can either block or facilitate practical counselling with clients. Examine these two cases and decide where the counsellor blocks and where they facilitate listening with understanding. What worked and what could be done to improve the counselling session?

1 • Terry

TERRY *(Arrives for the counselling session. His trousers, jacket and shirt are wet. He is shivering and sneezing a lot. His face is pale and he talks in a croaking voice.)*:

COUNSELLOR: Good morning, Terry. Now where did we leave off last time?

TERRY: I'd like to do something about these wet … first …

COUNSELLOR: Ah, yes, I remember you had a fixation about your mother and I believe I successfully diagnosed that you suffered from delusions about your body … Yes, yes, that's right you are fixated and deluded.

TERRY: I can't think about what you are saying this morning until I warm up … and dry off a bit …

COUNSELLOR: You see, Terry, what you are saying, do you? You are showing just how unable you are to face reality in these counselling sessions. Now the reality is …

TERRY: I am wet.

COUNSELLOR: Indeed. So anxious to avoid facing your fear of your mother you are prepared to get wet. You can only think about maintaining your fixation so you delude yourself.

TERRY: I am cold as well.

Listening with Understanding

FACILITATING	BLOCKING
● Checking that what clients say is what they mean.	■ Putting own interpretation on what client says without checking with client.
● Understanding the tone and mood of client statements/views/opinions.	■ Disregarding the tonality or mood of client statements/views/opinions.
● Linking with and using language of client.	■ Using technical jargon or esoteric language that baffles/confuses client.
● Spotting key phrases used by clients.	■ Ignoring/failing to notice key phrases used by clients.
● Hearing changes in client emotions or mood.	■ 'Deaf' to changes in client emotions or mood.
● Attending to thoughts that matter to client.	■ Directing clients to attend to what counsellor thinks.
● Discovering what clients make of their situation or what it means to them.	■ Telling clients what they should make of their situation and/or what it must mean to them.
● Respecting clients' struggle to make progress in understanding at their own pace.	■ Urging the client to go at a pace that suits the counsellor's understanding of the client.
● Confirming with clients that you understand them.	■ Assuming you understand clients.
● Confirming with clients that they understand you.	■ Assuming clients understand you.

COUNSELLOR: Cold and missing the warmth of your mother. Yes, problems of attachment and separation neuroses are evident, and that wet feeling, Terry — it all fits now.

TERRY: Does it? It still feels wet and cold to me. I need a hot drink to warm me up.

COUNSELLOR: No, I can assure you Terry, I have seen many cases such as yours. I am afraid you are suffering from early psychoneurotic anxiety through a mother fixation complex generating delusional thinking and flights from reality. *(Addressing Terry as if making a prize-giving speech)* Only a few minutes left till your time is up Terry. *(Counsellor looking at his watch and indicating his urgency to press on and get the session over)*

TERRY *(sounding utterly confused)*: Eh ... What?

COUNSELLOR: Now we understand each other, Terry, you must be feeling a little better now.

TERRY: Er? No. I need a hot drink and some dry clothes.

2 • Bernice

BERNICE *(arriving at office shouting and swearing and throwing coat down and kicking the chair)*:

COUNSELLOR: It looks like you have got a lot on your mind today, Bernice. *(Said in an interested but questioning tone)*

BERNICE: I'm damn bloody angry. So angry I could could shout ... I want to break something ... anything ... *(Takes a huge intake of breath and kicks chair again)*

COUNSELLOR *(mirrors Bernice's intake of breath and stretches arms and legs, matching the kick by client but much less aggressive)*: You must have a good reason for feeling the way you do ... so strong these feelings. I wonder what these feelings are like for you.

BERNICE *(moving out of the kicking and shouting and moving less fiercely and beginning to lower her voice)*: Oh, they just bubble away under the surface, sometimes for months and then like this morning I just explode, and it all comes tumbling out ...

COUNSELLOR: So you know when these feelings begin to bubble up and grow in their intensity inside you ... Is it a bit like a pressure cooker?

BERNICE: Yes, it's like that only I don't have a safety valve.

COUNSELLOR: You seem to know about these things, Bernice. What else can you tell me?

BERNICE: Well, they seem to be triggered off by thinking about nasty things.

COUNSELLOR: Can you tell me about these nasty things?

BERNICE: I can't ... really *(Hesitates, almost says something)*

COUNSELLOR: I remember having nasty thoughts and I didn't feel like talking about them ... yet, I kept having them. I understand if you need to keep them to yourself right now.

BERNICE: I do ... you're so understanding. *(Bernice seems much more relaxed and focused on examining the problem, her emotions have changed and are less volatile.)*

COUNSELLOR: Thanks . . . maybe we understand each other a bit better than we did five minutes ago ... I wonder if you notice any ways you seem to be different now.

BERNICE: I feel more calm and in control . . .

COUNSELLOR: Mmm ... I notice that as well ... calm and in control.

BERNICE: You know I really do want to get back at Vince. I'd like to hurt him the way he is hurting me.

COUNSELLOR: Is that something you feel you're going through now?

BERNICE: Yes, that is what this morning was all about. I was blazing angry.

COUNSELLOR: And you were hurting as well as being angry. That's one way of showing that you could be thinking nasty things.

BERNICE: It is ... sure ... but I want to do something about it ... I really do ...

COUNSELLOR: Sure, and what is it you would like to do something about?

BERNICE: Drugs, I'm not having drugs in my house.

COUNSELLOR: Have I got this right, Bernice? You're saying Vince is in some way connected with drugs in your house?

BERNICE: He has been at it for months now, but I have had enough. *(Pauses and sighs and tears run down her cheeks)*

COUNSELLOR: Yes ... it must be difficult for you ... take your time . . . just tell me what you need to tell me at your own pace ...

Analysis

In the first case the counsellor failed to practise any of the principles of observing or listening with understanding. There were things the counsellor did that he should not have done and others he did not do that he should have done. Let's first of all examine what he did do that he should not have done. You can see from the case example that the counsellor unwittingly engaged in blocking progress in the counselling session. Did you notice the blocking the counsellor was practising?

The counsellor:

▶ took no notice of Terry being wet and cold
▶ ignored requests made by Terry
▶ reinterpreted what Terry said to suit his view of the case; failed to listen
▶ completely failed to observe Terry's needs
▶ distorted what Terry said
▶ spoke in jargon and used language inappropriate for Terry
▶ ignored Terry's confusion
▶ pressed on at too fast a pace
▶ tried to make progress prematurely
▶ assumed he understood Terry
▶ disregarded whether or not Terry understood him.

Now go back to the second case and notice the way the counsellor worked differently with Bernice.

The counsellor:

▶ acknowledged Bernice and the state she was in
▶ mirrored and matched some of Bernice's movements and matched her breathing pattern
▶ slowed the tempo down gradually in the way she spoke to Bernice
▶ listened attentively
▶ used similar language to Bernice, used similar tonality and emphasis on same words as Bernice, eg. "calm and in control"
▶ checked that she understood Bernice
▶ confirmed that she was understood by Bernice
▶ did not disregard the things Bernice wanted to talk about

▶ built a 'bridge' to link Bernice's feelings, thoughts and behaviour

▶ connected what Bernice was feeling and doing when she arrived with what she wanted to do in the counselling session

▶ progressed at a pace acceptable to Bernice

▶ avoided getting stuck

▶ combined observing and listening with understanding

▶ built and maintained rapport

▶ asked Bernice for help

▶ observed Bernice had changed and drew her attention to it.

Practice

●

Meet your counselling group or a colleague and practise observing and listening with understanding. Take turns role playing the client and counsellor. Make the first role play a case where the counsellor breaks the rules of observing and listening with understanding or simply fails to put them into practice. What was it like for the client? The counsellor?

Now carry out another set of role plays, this time expressing the essential skills involved in observing and listening with understanding. What happened this time? Again notice what it was like for the client and the counsellor.

Finally, discuss amongst yourselves or with your clients what seems most helpful in your counselling when you are observing and listening with understanding.

Make notes of the observing and listening with understanding skills that you wish to continue using, those you will continue to develop, the ones you will discontinue using, and those you will acquire and use.

Summary

●

Observing and listening with understanding are essential skills for competent counsellors. They are of practical value at many levels when working with clients in counselling. Observing what clients say, think, feel and do and the way they walk and talk are all skills that counsellors need to become aware of. The way they do this is by improving their observing skills. In addition to observing, counsellors should develop their abilities to listen with understanding to their clients. Listening with understanding complements competent observing, and is an active process, where counsellor and client work towards knowing what the problem or difficulty is and what might be done about it. Listening with understanding goes hand in hand with observing, and both take place over the whole period of time clients are in counselling. During this time counsellors engage in learning to listen to and listening to learn from their clients. Observing and listening with understanding are often combined with other practical counselling skills such as making appropriate openings, starting counselling sessions and building rapport.

Clearly, it is important that we acquire and retain a wide range of skills which can be integrated in our helping and counselling with clients. Observing and listening with understanding can make a significant contribution to this effort. There needs to be sufficient preparation and practice of observing and listening with understanding skills. Using these skills reduces the risk of blocking clients and increases the prospect of facilitating their progress through counselling.

Chapter 9

COUNSELLING WITH PERSONAL INFORMATION

Preparation

●

Clients suffer because they do not know how to satisfy their needs. They believe they either lack the information to satisfy these needs or do not know how to access and use the information that would help them better manage themselves. Clients who come to me for counselling are often mixed up and disorganized in their thinking, stressed, anxious and angry. Sometimes they are not sure what they are feeling and thinking and unclear what their problem is, or what they are doing and why it is causing them problems. Yet these very clients often have the information which would help them to understand their problem. They have the information that would help them understand, change and satisfy their needs.

Other clients have just too much information. The problem here is they do not know how to organize their personal information to help themselves. A bit like an amateur juggler, they have all the balls they need to perform an impressive juggling act. However, they do not know how to keep the balls in the air. They somehow can't quite discover the secret of how to co-ordinate the throwing of the balls, the movement of the hands, the balance of the body with the concentration on keeping the sequence of movements going so the balls do not collide or just simply fall down. One of the fascinating things about jugglers is that they start with the most that they can handle with ease, and add to it, gradually and progressively building up so that they can juggle more and more balls and still make it look easy. I find that clients who have too much information, and are troubled in some way special to them, often have something in common. They are trying to juggle too many balls at once. They are not only suffering from not satisfying their needs. They also have too much information, and they don't know how to manage it. It reminds me of a woman who had three counselling sessions with me.

At first she talked about the problems she had with her husband and her children. To some extent this was a true picture. However, in her attempts to satisfy her needs for recognition, and to exert more control over her life and receive affection, she had loaded herself up with too much information. She ran the house, cooked the meals, did the garden, and had a job. She started an Open University course and attended seminars in London once every six weeks. She commuted to visit her sister at weekends. In addition, she had met a man on a course who she had a lot in common with, and she tried to spend her 'spare time' with him. On top of all this she was mixed up over her feelings and the facts of the situation. She had certain feelings about the facts and the facts gave her certain feelings. She had lots of information, personal information that mattered to her and her life, but it was all tangled up and she needed to sort it out. She was suffering from a surge of information she could no longer manage.

Information can be hot or cold. There is feeling information, about the emotions, the specific personal experience of the client, how it feels right now to be the client. So for people in counselling, information often has a lot of emotional content. For others, it has factual content.

Counsellors, therefore, have several tasks in working with clients. They should enable clients to discover if they have enough personal information to understand their problems. They should also make it possible for clients to decide if they have too much information and how they might sort it out so they can better understand themselves. In doing so, counsellors should be vigilant as to whether or not the client is working with 'hot' or 'cold' information: information pertaining to feelings or information pertaining to facts. Counsellors should always be alert to the appropriateness of their own use of counselling skills in these circumstances. There will be times when the counsellor needs to make a response or an intervention, or lead the client, by focusing on feelings, and at other times it will be more appropriate to emphasize the facts.

However, remember it is the personal information of the client that is of fundamental importance, both to them and to the counselling session. This does not mean that we cannot or should not introduce new information or empower clients to reduce the amount of information they need to work with in counselling sessions. What it does mean is that the counsellor is the person who has the responsibility of understanding, with the client, their understanding of themselves. Sharing, gathering, accessing and ordering personal information opens the door to a fuller understanding of the client. Finally, in working with information, counsellors should be clear about where they are with their clients during each part of the counselling session. Are we helping clients gather information to assess their problem? Are we facilitating or blocking clients in their efforts to sort out the personal information in their lives? Are we consciously introducing new and fresh information that leads clients to assess or reassess their problem and see it in a different way? Whatever the particular circumstances for each client, never forget it is the client's information and understanding of that information which is important to assess, explore and act upon in counselling sessions. Personal information belongs to the client and it needs to be respected at all times. It is this personal information that counsellors work with in counselling sessions.

Case Examples

1 • Maggie

COUNSELLOR: Now Maggie, what seems to be your problem?

MAGGIE: I can't stop spending money. Whenever I see anything I have got to have it. I can't go out of the house but I buy things, especially what's advertised on telly. *(Beginning to open up and tell the counsellor more since last meeting, having established good rapport)*

COUNSELLOR: What does your husband say about all this? It's not right, is it Maggie? You're being bad. *(Said very seriously and in moralizing tone)*

MAGGIE: I don't know what you mean. *(Suddenly Maggie is quiet, saying little, and becoming annoyed with the counsellor.)*

COUNSELLOR: Look, its perfectly simple. Your husband works very hard for his money and there you are spending it all. It won't do.

MAGGIE: No, you look, I have no money of my own. I don't know how to make the money I have last. I spend ages trying to figure it out and then I get in a spin, my mind goes blank. There is so much to pay, groceries, rent, school lunches, clothes, spending money. I just need to sort things out. Every time I see an advert I think I need to go out and buy what I see. You just don't know what it is like.

COUNSELLOR: Of course I do. We have all been in that position, Maggie. You see something, you want it, you buy it. Then you realize you have spent money you can't afford.

MAGGIE: Oh, you are just confusing me more with this ... I mean, some of what you say is right but it doesn't feel right to me. I know something else is wrong and I can't talk to my husband about it ... It all needs sorting out. I thought I was getting somewhere with it last week but now you really have set me wondering ... Maybe I need more money. Maybe I can't manage money, I don't know ... I don't even know why I spend so much, it is so upsetting at times. *(During this flood of feelings and questions about facts Maggie implicitly has said to the counsellor that the assumptions he is making about her are incorrect. The counsellor ignores all of what she says and also the implications in what she has said.)*

COUNSELLOR: Right, my girl. Next Monday I want you and your husband in here and we are going to get to the bottom of this. Your husband can help you control your spending and that will be the best way to deal with this one.

MAGGIE: Not on your sweet life. It won't change a thing, and the last person I want to be with in these sessions is him.

2 • Mike

COUNSELLOR: Come in Mike, glad you could make it. Now what seems to be the problem?

MIKE: I don't rightly know. But I keep wanting sex with any woman I see.

COUNSELLOR: Any woman?

MIKE: Well, that's not quite true. But I want to have sex with lots of women.

COUNSELLOR: Old, young and in-between?

MIKE: I find it is mainly the older ones.

COUNSELLOR: How old is older?

MIKE: You know, about 40 or so.

COUNSELLOR: And how does it feel knowing you want sex with older women?

MIKE: A bit of me feels really excited and another is saying I'm dirty and then I feel guilty.

COUNSELLOR: So you feel guilty and good at the same time when you are thinking about sex with older women.

MIKE: No, I feel good first of all, then I quickly feel guilty.

COUNSELLOR: Just thinking about it …

MIKE: Yeh, just thinking about it, seeing the pictures in my head. But thinking about it confuses me because I don't know if I am supposed to think and feel these things.

COUNSELLOR: I can imagine it is confusing not knowing how you should feel. How would you like to feel when you are thinking these things about these older women?

MIKE: I don't want to feel guilty.

COUNSELLOR: I appreciate you don't want to feel guilty, but what would you like to feel and think?

MIKE: I want to get rid of this little nagging voice in my head.

COUNSELLOR: And this nagging voice is saying something to you?

MIKE: Yeh, it's the one that says I am dirty and doing bad things and I should be punished for having these feelings and thoughts.

COUNSELLOR: How long have you known this voice, Mike?

MIKE: About two years now.

COUNSELLOR: So you know it quite well.

MIKE: Too bloody well.

COUNSELLOR: And you know what it says, and how it makes you feel. I would like your help in understanding and getting to know this voice a little bit better, if that is OK with you, Mike.

MIKE: Sure, I want to know more as well.

COUNSELLOR: So we want to know more about this voice in your head. We know what it says and how you feel. What does the voice sound like? I mean, if you really listened very carefully I wonder what it sounds like.

MIKE: It sounds very stern and angry with me and it has … I know this might sound funny … but it has a kind of foreign accent and it's saying, "You will be punished. You are evil. You are unclean ..."

COUNSELLOR: Mike, I would like to thank you for helping me to understand this voice. I would like to know if we could hear this voice in a different way. Maybe it would say the same things but sing them in a sweet and soothing way or maybe you would like to try changing the accent or words. Where do you think it might be best to begin? ...

Analysis

These two case examples illustrate how counsellors can empower or prevent clients from discovering personal information. In Case One the counsellor was only concerned with the information he thought appropriate to the client. Repeatedly, the counsellor prevented the client providing information about herself and her difficulties. In addition, the counsellor continued to assume what was best for the client. This is one of the classic errors of counselling. Not once did the counsellor check with the client whether these assumptions were correct. Indeed, if the counsellor had been more vigilant, he would have detected quite easily that the assumptions being made about Maggie were wildly inaccurate. In a nutshell, the counsellor was working with counsellor information and ignoring client information.

In Case Two, the counsellor was radically different. First of all the counsellor made very few assumptions about the client or about the information that was required by the client. In fact it was made clear on at least one occasion that the client could help the counsellor by providing personal information about himself. When the client provided the personal information, it was evident that the counsellor helped him to untangle and reorder the information. Sensitive questioning by the counsellor, and checking with the client, led to new client information emerging that formed the basis for the counsellor asking Mike how they might begin to work on it together and change the words or voices he heard in his head.

In Case One, the counsellor had a ready-made 'solution' to Maggie's personal problems. In Case Two the counsellor needed information and so did the client. The counsellor worked with the

Questions Useful for Discovering and Reordering Client Information

Once you have created, established and retained rapport, and begun to listen to clients, you should find it helpful to discover the kind of information that is important to them and how it might be reordered for use in counselling sessions. These questions, when used sensitively alongside your other counselling skills, are potent in revealing personal information that is relevant to clients in counselling.

HOT INFORMATION	COLD INFORMATION
Information that deals with emotions/feelings	**Information that deals with facts/data**
● "How do you feel about that?"	■ "Where did this happen?"
● "What feeling does that give you?"	■ "Who was present/absent at the time?"
● "When you have this experience what is it like?"	■ "When did it/does it happen?"
● "How does that affect you/them?"	■ "When does it not happen?"
● "I wonder how it feels when you think about that as you look back/now/as you look forward."	■ "How does it happen/not happen?"
	■ "What makes you think this is a problem?"
● "Can you help me understand the emotions you are experiencing now?"	■ "How much better/worse is it in these situations?"
● "I would be interested to learn how you feel when . . ."	■ "What is it about him/her/them/ the situation that . . .?"
● "How do you know when you are upset?"	■ "How do you stop it happening?"
● "How would I/he/she/they know you felt . . .?"	■ "Which people are involved?"
● "What are you feeling now?"	■ "How will you know when this problem has been solved?"
● "What would you like to feel instead?"	■ "How long have you experienced this?"

client accessing hot and cold information, finding out how the client felt and how long he had experienced his difficulty. The counsellor also validated the information they would need if they were to make further progress in their counselling sessions together.

Practice/Assignment
●

With a colleague, or in a group, look over these two case examples again. Identify the ways in which you could have better used practical counselling skills in Case One. Which specific things would you have done to make it possible for the client to get access to and work with her personal information? How would you have gone about counselling the client using hot and cold information? Where would you have kept things the same and where changed them in Case Two? Why?

When you have done this spend some time role playing the cases over again. Each person should play the part of the client and the counsellor in the two cases. Be prepared to experiment with your ability to empower your client to access hot and cold information. Also combine a number of the previous practical counselling skills in these role plays. Make them as near 'real' as you can. Go ahead.

How did you get on? What specific skills are working well for you and which ones still need to be strengthened and refined? How easily were you able to combine a number of counselling skills when you were working with your clients? How conscious were you of using them? Which counsellings skills are now becoming 'second nature' to you? Write out or draw a map of the counselling skills you have acquired so far and the ones you will continue to work on in the future and how you will do this.

As well as reflecting on your own performance in these role plays, you can benefit greatly by getting feedback from those people who played clients to you as counsellor. Similarly, give constructive feedback to those who played counsellors when you were role playing the client.

Now make a final statement about your current level of practical counselling skills. Be sure to make specific references to skills building, listening skills and ability, and your competence in enabling clients to work with information that is personal and relevant to them.

Review
●

Counselling with the personal information of the client is critical for building rapport and making progress in counselling sessions. Clients need to have sufficient information if they are to make choices about the way they want to live their lives. There are times when it is information overload that is the difficulty for clients. They have so much going on in their minds and feelings that they cannot think straight or take action to solve their problems or change their situation. Where there is insufficient information, counsellors influence clients by enabling them to obtain information that is relevant to make personal progress in counselling sessions. Conversely, in a situation where clients have too much information, counsellors influence them by enabling them to reduce or reorganize their personal information. Personal information may be hot or cold. Hot information is concerned with the client's emotions and feelings. Cold information is related to facts and structuring the personal data of clients. Counsellors provide clients with the opportunity to access their personal information. Clients use their personal information as a way of reviewing their past, their present and how they might change in the future. We aim to combine a number of practical counselling skills such as rapport building and careful listening when we are working with the personal information of clients.

Chapter 10

THE POWER OF FEEDBACK

Preparation

Feedback is powerful. Without it we would not be able to survive. The child who begins to learn to walk doesn't usually succeed right away. Walking usually involves a process of feedback. The child learns to sit up, to crawl, to pull itself up, to stand, to take its first step and then it is off — walking. Alongside this are the child's parents or relatives urging them on, giving guidance and lots of support. Sounds very simple, doesn't it? However, all the time the child has been working with feedback to solve the problem of how to walk. Working out how to sit, how to crawl, how to stand, how to walk. The working out depended on five aspects of feedback.

1 Feedback from the physiological and muscular activity in its body;
2 Feedback from thinking;
3 Feedback from feeling;
4 Feedback from seeing the external environment;
5 Feedback on how well it is doing.

Depending on the results of feedback, the way the feedback was experienced, thought about, felt, processed and acted upon, the child made progress in walking. If not, it would set out and try again. The child would try again and again in a number of different ways until it succeeded in learning to walk. Now very soon after this, walking comes easily and becomes natural. As people grow into adults they usually forget how they managed to learn how to walk. The feedback is still there but the individual seems to act on it automatically. Without the knowledge of that feedback and the way it is to be used, walking would not be possible.

Another example of the power of feedback is learning to drive a car. What happens? You enter the car and all these unfamiliar controls are pointed out to you by the driving instructor. Each control is explained: how it operates different parts of the car. Eventually you start to drive the car, attempting to link what you have been told about the controls with actually carrying out the act of driving. To begin with you make some errors. Maybe you forget to signal or to stop in the right place. Or maybe you brake too suddenly or too late, or forget which direction you are steering the car in, or fail to notice the other vehicles on the road or to take avoiding action. You could be upset, angry, anxious and even thinking of giving up driving forever. There seems so many things to learn about driving.

Learner drivers know they are driving well or badly because of the feedback they receive from their driving instructors. Once they can integrate all of the relevant feedback from the controls of the car and the traffic conditions, they are in a better position to drive well. Until they can do this, they run the risks of accidents. The constructive use of feedback enables them to drive responsibly within their current level of driving skill.

Feedback and Clients

●

Counselling clients with feedback is like learning to walk, or driving a car. Counsellors need to be aware of the feedback that will empower clients to understand their problems and the ways in which they are maintaining their personal difficulties. Clients should learn about the way they are going about trying to solve their problems and the results this has for themselves and others. Counsellors provide feedback on how they understand clients are currently thinking, feeling and experiencing the problems they are facing in their lives.

Feedback can also be used to enable clients to consider changing the way they think, feel and behave in the future, in different situations. Counsellors who provide effective feedback to clients are helping them to learn.

Therefore the quality of feedback counsellors provide to clients plays a large part in the practice of practical counselling. Indeed, the kind of feedback clients receive from counsellors can inhibit or facilitate progress in counselling sessions. We need to be aware of the types of feedback that counsellors give to their clients that

USEFUL FEEDBACK	FUTILE FEEDBACK
● Repeating key client words or phrases.	■ Ignoring key client words or phrases.
● Reflecting client feelings.	■ Telling client how/what they should feel.
● Reflecting client thinking.	■ Telling client how/what they should think.
● Reflecting what client is doing.	■ Telling client what they should do.
● Reflecting how client is behaving.	■ Telling clients how to behave. Counsellor does not acknowledge client behaviour.
● Paraphrasing current thoughts/feelings/behaviour of client.	■ Listing counsellor priorities to exclusion of client priorities.
● Summarizing client views.	■ Replacing client view with counsellor view.
● Summarizing client feelings.	■ Refusing to summarize client feelings.
● Summarizing client actions.	■ Refusing to summarize client actions.
● Counsellors say how they feel about client/situation.	■ Counsellors fail to express how they feel about client/situation.
● Counsellors say what they think about client/situation.	■ Counsellors fail to express what they think about client/situation.
● Counsellors express hunches about their understanding of client.	■ Counsellors do not express hunches about their understanding of client.
● Checking consequences of clients' thoughts/feelings/actions.	■ Counsellors do not check their understanding of consequences for client.
● Checking clients' understanding of their thoughts/feelings/actions.	■ Counsellor does not check clients' understanding of their thoughts/feelings/actions.

are useful for them, and feedback that is futile and unhelpful. Study the different forms of feedback on page 119. Once you are familiar with them examine the two case examples. Pay particular attention to identifying and recognizing when the counsellors provided futile feedback and when they engaged in giving useful feedback to the client. Which specific forms of feedback are relevant for clients in these two cases? Why?

Case Examples

1 • Trudy

TRUDY: I came here because I feel ugly and depressed. I feel suicidal.

COUNSELLOR: You shouldn't feel like that, a young woman like you.

TRUDY: No, I mean it. The thoughts of not going on keep running around and around in my head ... It's getting worse. I used to be able to turn them off using my will power ... It was a struggle. I think I am dirty and useless.

COUNSELLOR: Don't think like that, it is unhealthy for you. You ought to be thinking how you can go out and enjoy yourself. What you should do is go out. Get a boy friend. Get a hobby.

TRUDY *(bursts into tears)*:   That's the trouble. All my bother is through a guy and I met him doing my hobby ... I'm a keen ballroom dancer ... I don't want to see men or go dancing again.

COUNSELLOR: Mm . . . Now come on, Trudy, it's not half as bad as that. You must see things differently. It's all over, someone you met. There's lots of other men who like ballroom dancing. You have to get things in perspective ... sort your priorities out. What I suggest is this. You get yourself out and down to the ballroom, enrol in some lessons, you can meet lots of other men there and soon your troubles will be over.

TRUDY: I don't think you understand. I am pregnant.

COUNSELLOR: Well that's quite a different matter. Why didn't you say so before now?

TRUDY: I don't know what to do. I am so mixed up.

COUNSELLOR: It is perfectly clear what you must do. You must have it.

TRUDY: It? *(Sounding utterly dismayed and despondent)*

COUNSELLOR: The ... your child. No wonder you are feeling sorry for yourself. You have to have this child. It had no part in your pranks and pleasures. It is innocent. Your needs have to come second at present. What you can be doing is making arrangements for the child to be adopted.

TRUDY: I think you're missing the point. *(Sounding flat but concise, coherent and lucid)*

COUNSELLOR: The point. The point. What are you driving at now?

TRUDY: I suffer from haemophilia and I am terrified of having a baby. You're just making me feel guilty telling me to have the child. I want to talk to someone else: someone that can help me understand how I really feel, someone who might let me sort out my thinking. Maybe then I could decide what I can do.

COUNSELLOR: That is what I am supposed to be here for ...

TRUDY: Sorry, but I am desperate. I want to see someone else. I really need help.

2 • Robbie

ROBBIE: You have no idea what it is like living with this secret.

COUNSELLOR: Secret? *(Said in an accepting but slightly questioning tone)*

ROBBIE: Yes, it's been on my mind for months now — ever since I found out ... *(Voice trails off and stops after saying this)*

COUNSELLOR: And you have been thinking about it for some time now. *(Said as a confirmation of what client has said)*

ROBBIE: I feel it's bursting to come out but I am afraid. Yet it's so painful ... I feel it right here. *(Points to throat)*

COUNSELLOR: I wonder if you are suffering from wanting to share your secret and suffering if you don't? And that is painful. *(Passes hand across chin)*

ROBBIE: Oh yes, I am suffering. You're dead right. It's like waiting for a funeral.

COUNSELLOR: Robbie, I noticed when you were talking just now that you used the phrases "dead right" and "waiting for a funeral". I wonder if there is anything in what you say that has to do with your secret? *(Pauses and waits for Robbie to reply; pause lasts for three minutes)*

ROBBIE: Eh no ... not really ... I ... well maybe. I feel it might be
...

COUNSELLOR: I feel you are trying to tell me something, Robbie, something that you have thought about a great deal, and maybe you've been worried about it as well ... It sounds as if it is difficult ... just take your time. *(Last phrase said in a slower, deliberate manner)*

ROBBIE: Cancer. I have cancer. *(Blurts it out to counsellor)*

COUNSELLOR: Am I right in thinking that this was the secret that you have been wrestling with all this time.?

ROBBIE *(crying and sighing)*:   Yes. Now at last it's out in the open. Oh God, it feels I've needed to tell someone for so long. I can't really express how difficult it has been for me.

COUNSELLOR *(counsellor sighs similar to Robbie's sigh)*:   I reckon nobody really knows what you have been going through and now you have let it out for the first time, maybe it says something else to you.

ROBBIE: It's saying so many things now. I don't know where to start. When I look back and think of the time I have wasted.

COUNSELLOR: Where are you now?

ROBBIE *(sounding slightly surprised)*:   Uh ... here with you in the room.

COUNSELLOR: And how are you feeling now?

ROBBIE: Tired but relieved.

COUNSELLOR: You're tired and relieved. Anything else?

ROBBIE: Guilty.

COUNSELLOR: Guilty ... about what?

ROBBIE: I think I have been selfish and just thinking of myself. I have my wife and two daughters to think about as well. It would destroy them to find out about my ... illness ... I mean how could I tell them about ... me having ... cancer?

COUNSELLOR: Robbie, I want to make sure I understand you, so can I check something out with you? I hear you saying you would like to find some way of telling your wife and children about your cancer but you're not sure if that would be a good thing to do. Have I got that right?

ROBBIE: That's right, but I would rather tell Brenda *(Robbie's wife)* and then we could discuss how best to let the children know.

COUNSELLOR: So you think you would rather work things out with Brenda first before anything else.

ROBBIE: I know I would prefer to do it that way. But as I said, I am afraid of the effects it would have on Brenda.

COUNSELLOR: OK, Robbie. Just as you managed to think about your cancer and found the courage to tell me about it, I wonder if you could tell me how you would feel telling Brenda.

ROBBIE: I would feel better ... I know I would ... I ... would feel ... I'd get rid of this guilt ... I'm keeping something away from her. We have always been open and honest with each other.

COUNSELLOR: You would feel better. I'm guessing, and tell me if I am wrong, but you seem to want to tell Brenda but you don't know how to ...

ROBBIE: No, you're right. This damn thing in my throat ... it's spreading and I have to get an operation quick ... I'm not sure if I will be able to speak again or maybe it will get into my lungs. I've got to tell Brenda ...

COUNSELLOR: Let's take these two things one at a time: how much you know about your cancer, and telling Brenda. Is that all right with you?

ROBBIE: I only know I have got cancer of the throat and it's spreading fast. Other than that I have read some stories about other people that ended up dying with it ... I am afraid ... it will be the same for me ... Then it's the end, and well ... *(Sobs and then is silent)*

COUNSELLOR: I believe you are being brave about your own suffering Robbie . . . and I notice that you are trying to protect Brenda and the children. Had you ever thought that Brenda or the children might want to face this together with you?

ROBBIE: Oh, I know they would. They always have stood by me. I'm the same with them. We're a 'strong together' family. Whenever there is a crisis we rally round each other. It's really great having that feeling of someone close to you ... someone who really cares ... you know what I mean.

COUNSELLOR: Mmm ... and Brenda and the children care about you and you care about them. I'd like to ask you if you know what Brenda would want you to do about your secret.

ROBBIE: She would like me to tell her about it ... the cancer, and I would like to tell her . . .

COUNSELLOR: So you both want the same thing ... have I understood you, Robbie?

ROBBIE: Yes, we want the same thing. I know that now.

COUNSELLOR: Robbie we have come a long way together in this session. You had a secret which you thought about a great deal and worried about. You have been able to share your secret with me and told me you have cancer of the throat. You have been brave and tried to protect your wife and family from this but you feel guilty and you would like to share what you think you know with them. But first of all you would like to be able to let your wife Brenda know, and you know that she would like to know as she cares about you and so do your children. You feel strong in facing things together. If there is anything I have left out or distorted in any way I'd like you to help me put that right …

Analysis

In Case One, the counsellor engaged in providing lots of futile feedback to the client. Trudy tried to express her thoughts and feelings and what she thought was her problem. However, the counsellor ignored her attempts and prevented her from telling her story. Moreover, the counsellor replaced Trudy's priorities with her own and did not check her understanding of the client's thoughts, feelings or behaviour. Worryingly, the counsellor imposed her own interpretation of Trudy's difficulties on the case and lectured her on her past behaviour and what she should do in the future. The counsellor refused to summarize the present position in counselling, or check whether this was how the client understood the position. Hunches were not made explicit by the counsellor. Instead, the counsellor expressed certainty about what Trudy's difficulties were and what should be done about them. Even when it became clear that the counsellor had grossly misunderstood and misrepresented Trudy's difficulties, the counsellor made no effort to readjust her position or feedback or concede that she had been wrong. All in all, Case One demonstrates most of the pitfalls of providing futile feedback to clients.

One possibility is that the counsellor was simply having an 'off day'. Alternatively, she was insensitive to the client, ill-prepared, insufficiently skilful, and only interested in her own view of the problem: moralizing about what was wrong and what should be done to put things right. Which alternative do you support? Why?

Case Two was handled quite differently by the counsellor. There was significant evidence of useful feedback by the counsellor. Remember, Robbie came to the counselling session with a secret, and apparently not sure if he wanted to tell anyone about it. Or if he did tell someone, he was not sure whom he should tell. We know now that the 'secret' was cancer of the throat. So what went on in this counselling session? What changed things?

Specifically, the counsellor did repeat key words and phrases used by the client. She reflected back the thoughts and feelings of the client to him and what they seemed to be doing. The counsellor also paraphrased at specific intervals what Robbie was saying and checked her understanding with him. In addition, the counsellor paid attention to Robbie's understanding of his secret, and his thoughts and feelings about it. At times the counsellor invited more expression from Robbie, wondering what it would be like if he took one course of action or another. At some points in the session, the counsellor expressed how she felt about what Robbie was saying and drew attention to some observations made about the way Robbie was describing how he felt. Several times the counsellor checked some hunches and corrected these with the help of Robbie. At these times in the session, the counsellor clearly communicated that Robbie would be able to contribute to the progress of the counselling session. At no time in the session did the counsellor replace Robbie's views with her own views or opinions. However, the gentle but consistent checking and the hunches of the counsellor helped to 'move' Robbie into seeing his situation as one where he would like to be able to share the discovery that he had throat cancer with his wife and maybe his children. The session ended with a summary by the counsellor which was checked with Robbie for any changes he might want to make to it.

A number of additional practical counselling skills were used by the counsellor in the session with Robbie. What do you think they were? Whereabouts in the session did they occur?

Practice
●

Find a partner or colleague. Each of you should play the role of the counsellor and the client. First of all, carry out a role play where you give futile feedback as a counsellor and experience it as the client. Reverse roles and do the same again. Break off from the role play and then share and compare your experiences.

What was it like being the counsellor who gave futile feedback? How did the client experience receiving futile feedback? What does receiving futile feedback do to the client/the counselling session? What particular help is needed by the counsellor who engages in giving futile feedback to clients?

Next time you are working with real clients, make a mental note of the kind of feedback you are giving them. Remember to check with your clients the quality and usefulness of the feedback you give them.

Review
●

Providing high quality and useful feedback is essential for productive practical counselling. People use feedback all the time, from their physiology and muscles, in the way they think, feel and behave, and the way they deal with feedback from the external environment. Practical counselling aims to utilize feedback for the benefit of clients in counselling. Counsellors provide, draw attention to, and select the kind of feedback that they believe is appropriate for clients. The way counsellors do this, and the content of the feedback they give to clients, may be futile or useful. Futile feedback is generally counter-productive to the purposes of practical counselling. It makes it difficult, if not impossible, for clients to make progress in their counselling sessions. It is one of the responsibilities of counsellors to ensure that they provide their clients with useful feedback. Useful feedback enables counsellors to maintain rapport with clients, check that they have been understood, and focus on what the client has been saying, thinking and doing. Clients benefit from useful feedback by appreciating that they are understood and that the counsellor also has views, hunches and feelings about them and the alternative possible ways their problems may be understood. It is sometimes said that the power of feedback can open 'the eyes, ears, heart and mind of clients'. In this sense, the counsellor provides useful feedback in order that clients can better understand themselves and what they might begin to do to overcome problems, reorganize their experience, or change their personal circumstances.

I become what I choose and I choose what I become
WILL SCHUTZ
We are a bundle of habits
WILLIAM JAMES

Chapter 11

CHOOSING & CHANGING

Preparation

●

A famous Zen story gives us a clear idea of the importance of choosing and changing for clients in practical counselling. The story tells of a monk who is chased by a tiger and jumps off a cliff to avoid it. The monk hangs over the cliff, clinging to a branch from a withering tree, just out of range of the tiger's powerful jaws and claws. The monk has a number of choices. He could pull himself up from the branch and face the tiger. He could try to hang on to the branch. He could let go of the branch. Or he could think of something else to do. In fact this is what he did. He started to sing a song. And as he sang, the tiger became enchanted and fell fast asleep. The monk pulled himself up onto the top of the cliff again and escaped.

I find this story fascinating. It has parallels for many clients in counselling. Clients often find themselves in the monk's situation. They can face up to situations they are avoiding or find difficulty in dealing with directly. They can hang on to the way they have been thinking, feeling and behaving about their problems. They can let go of the way they have tended to think and feel and go about solving their difficulties and the experiences they have. They have choices. Some of these choices may be unattractive to them. Some choices may frustrate and fail to satisfy their personal needs. However, they are still choices.

The choices clients make are sometimes the ones that create and maintain their personal problems. Sometimes making one choice and acting on it solves a problem in one area of their lives but creates difficulties in others. Like the monk, they can temporarily stave off the tiger, but end up hanging over a precipice of another problem. Others learn to do something entirely different and are inspired to make new and novel choices to satisfy their needs. Up to then, the choices clients have been making have not been satisfying their personal needs. This is one of the main reasons clients come to counselling. Another reason clients come to counselling is that they seem to engage in making the same choices, thinking the same way, feeling the same feelings and behaving in habitual ways that prevent them from making significant personal changes in their lives. Viewed from this perspective, clients create their own problems in their efforts to satisfy their personal needs. They are hanging on to the branch of the withering tree. They appear to be, or believe they are, or are, unaware of other choices available to them.

Uncovering Choosing

In practical counselling, the counsellor has the task of enabling clients to uncover the choices they are making in their lives, and to examine the consequences this has for them. Curiously enough, we are not aware of many of the things we think, say, do and feel. In this sense we do not choose. We appear to react. We feel hungry, so we eat. We are thirsty, so we drink. We are tired, so we sleep. Many of our preconscious choices are satisfying and adaptive for us and help our body and mind to recover and resolve our problems 'spontaneously'.

However, our preconscious choices can often frustrate our needs and be maladaptive. We don't eat when we are hungry. We allow ourselves to become parched. We don't sleep when our body is tired. Our preconscious choices can also influence our emotional lives and interfere with our psychological needs. We get angry at someone for no apparent reason. We feel sad and can't explain why. We feel anxious and seem unable to associate it with any event. Sometimes these preconscious choices lead to minor problems such as disagreements and disturbed personal relationships. At other times, they are associated with consequences which are more serious, such as the loss of friends, broken marriages, alcohol and drug abuse, and physical illness. It is the counsellor's responsibility to help clients uncover and bring into awareness the preconscious choices that are frustrating and maladaptive for them. When preconscious choices are brought into conscious awareness then clients have the opportunity to consider how they

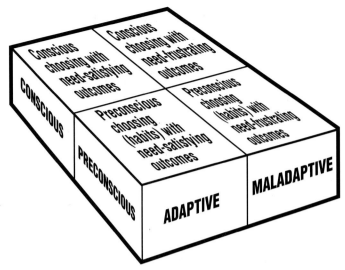

might think, feel and do things differently. They have the consciousness in which, with the counsellor, they discover and decide why, how, when and what they might choose to change in themselves, their situation, or others.

Choosing to Change

●

Choosing to change has two main points of significance for clients. They should know what changes they face and if these changes are likely to produce adaptive or maladaptive consequences. We work with clients at increasing their choosing and consciousness. In enabling clients to get in touch with their choosing we are creating the conditions in counselling where we draw attention to the way clients seem to choose, the choices they make, and the consequences this seems to have for them. Some of the time, clients are aware of their choosing and the counsellor can work with them on how much, how far, how little, or whether at all, they wish to change, and what specific changes they need to make in their lives. In these circumstances, it is also important for counsellors to be aware of what actually counts as change to their clients. One client found that simply changing the time she arrived home from work led to a decrease in family arguments. This change reduced the amount of frustration and aggression she experienced and made it possible for her to feel more secure and included in family life. Changes do not always need to be dramatic to have significant and satisfying results. In these instances, even a single or a few counselling sessions can be beneficial. However, I have found that enabling clients to become aware of their habits and their 'preconscious choosing' can take a little longer. In practical counselling, the counsellor helps clients to notice and become aware of their habits and those things they do, say, think and feel automatically. In uncovering habits, counsellors reveal clients to themselves. Making the preconscious conscious opens up new areas of choosing to clients. Uncovering makes new choices possible but not always probable.

I have found some clients wish to be aware of their habits, yet do not wish to change, or are not yet ready to make any changes for themselves or towards others in their lives. It is fundamental to practical counselling to accept and acknowledge the client's right not to change. Counsellors are in the influencing business. Yet it must be emphasized that their responsibility is to influence and create a climate in counselling where clients can increase the range of choices available to them. One choice clients have before them is to choose not to change. There are no such things as 'good' or 'bad' choices. There are only choices that are satisfying or frustrating experiences for clients. Choices have adaptive or maladaptive consequences for clients.

It is the client who chooses to change. Counsellors create the conditions whereby clients can expand their opportunities to change. Bringing personal habits into the awareness of clients helps to uncover the potential for new choosing. Uncovering means bringing what was preconscious into the conscious mind of clients. In the climate of caring, working with appropriate information, and careful listening, counsellors enable their clients to experience their choosing and face up to the changes they may want to make in their lives.

Challenging for Change
●

Change is challenging, and the counsellor should be prepared to challenge clients who wish to change. It is, however, crucial to get a clear perspective on what we mean by challenging clients and mobilizing the change process in practical counselling. I have found there are helpful and unhelpful ways of challenging clients in my efforts to facilitate change with them.

UNHELPFUL CHALLENGING	HELPFUL CHALLENGING
● Forcing clients to face their concerns.	■ Inviting clients to clarify their problem.
● Insisting clients do something else.	■ Asking how someone else would see their situation.
● Telling the client there are no other choices.	■ Wondering which part of the problem/concern client wants to work on.
● Playing the 'expert'.	■ Asking client for help.
● Suggesting things will not get better unless they change.	■ Listing client opportunities alongside their problems.
● Trying to be helpful too soon.	■ Waiting for appropriate moments.
● Offering solutions.	■ Finding out how client has managed difficulties in the past.
● Concentrating on past failures.	■ Congratulating client for overcoming problems in the past.
● Going over and over the problem in the same old way.	■ Looking at the problem from a different perspective.
	■ Asking clients to describe their strengths.
	■ Asking/inviting clients to summarize where they are in their thinking/feeling/doing.
● Assuming you know how clients think/feel about their choosing.	■ Summarizing how you feel/think about where clients are in their choosing.
● Assuming you know how/what client wants to change.	■ Summarizing where you feel/think the client wants to change.
	■ Checking with clients the changes they want/do not want to make.
	■ Expressing where you think/feel client is at present.
	■ Expressing your views/feelings about client problem/changes.
● Failing to check with client.	■ Encouraging client to doubt the current solutions.
● Encouraging client not to change.	■ Encouraging client to entertain change.

Case Examples

1 • Lloyd

COUNSELLOR: Now, Lloyd, isn't it about time you did something about these cars you keep stealing?

LLOYD: Don't know what you mean.

COUNSELLOR: Well, instead of stealing those cars at the weekends and joy-riding, you could be at home helping your poor mum.

LLOYD: Don't give me that.

COUNSELLOR: You don't have a choice, Lloyd. Unless you pull your socks up, mate, you're going to be in deep trouble.

LLOYD: What is this, eh? … I thought you were supposed to help me.

COUNSELLOR: If you take my advice you will stop going out Friday and Saturday nights and stay away from the centre of town on Sundays… that's what you have to do if you want to get yourself sorted out. I mean, look at your record. It is as long as my arm. You've no chance if you don't change.

LLOYD: You sound just like my mother. Are you two ganging up on me, then?

COUNSELLOR: I am at the end of my tether with you, Lloyd. Here I am trying to help you and what do I get? Abuse, nothing but abuse. You know that will never get you anywhere. It's too late for you isn't it? You're never going to change. What your mother must have had to put up with all these years … Such a charming woman. You know I have worked with people like you for years and I think I know a thing or two about what is best in these situations. Lloyd, are you listening to me?

LLOYD *(Lloyd stares out of the counselling room window in silence, and continues to do so until counselling session is over):*

2 • Arlene

COUNSELLOR: Hello again, Arlene, I am glad you decided to come to our session today. Arlene, it has been two weeks since we last met. At that time you said you had seen several doctors and that you were told you had bulimia and to you this meant you binged on food and then forced yourself to vomit it up again. Is that correct … did I understand you correctly?

ARLENE: That's right, but I also said that I seem to get worse when my relationships with people are not going right.

COUNSELLOR: Not going right? Could you clarify that for me?

ARLENE: Yes, I mean when I feel I want to be close to someone, to be friends, and then I get so worried I want to please them and then they back off and don't want to go out with me any more. When that happens I binge on burgers, cakes and biscuits, mainly cakes and burgers.

COUNSELLOR: Thanks, Arlene, you have now made that very clear to me. I wonder if it is the same for your male and female friends.

ARLENE: Oh, it really only happens with men.

COUNSELLOR: And you feel something that changes something and you worry about that. How does this appear to the male friends you have?

ARLENE: Oh, they would never understand. It's a feeling of emptiness and urgency and longing. It just doesn't go away until I stuff myself with food ...

COUNSELLOR: And then ...

ARLENE: I feel angry and make myself sick.

COUNSELLOR: Has there ever been a time when you found things were different?

ARLENE: Yes, things have been much better in the past when I could choose my friends and had much more control over how I feel, and control over my eating. I never binged then.

COUNSELLOR: I'd like to check out my understanding again with you, Arlene. I understand you to be saying you had control over your life in the past and you were able to choose the friends you had. You also had choices that made it possible for you to control your eating and you could control your feelings with friends. If you look at it this way, in those times you were in charge of your choosing — you were in control.

ARLENE: Yes, I do feel you understand what I am going through. It is a great relief to feel that someone understands me — after all this time. I can look at it the way you put it. I feel much better for some reason.

COUNSELLOR: How did you just do that?

ARLENE: Do what?

COUNSELLOR: Do what you did just now.

ARLENE: I thought you understood, and when I thought that I got relaxed feelings and not those empty and tense ones I told you about. I suppose I've got my control back ... for a time.

COUNSELLOR: If you could choose again and get more control for yourself what would you like to work on first?

ARLENE: Oh, those awful feelings ... I'd like better feelings when I am around men who are friends.

COUNSELLOR: Mmm ... better feelings ...

ARLENE: I think so, definitely, because the bad feelings come from men putting me down and then I binge and then it's a cycle after that.

COUNSELLOR: Arlene, I'd like to thank you again because I now know something else I didn't know a few moments ago. When you feel put down by men you get this bad feeling and the cycle of binging takes off. Is that where we are now?

ARLENE: We are at the stage where I realize I have managed to get control over my problem and feelings in the past and at those times I did not binge, and right now I am feeling relaxed and settled, and I am in control.

COUNSELLOR: I agree. I think that's where you are as well. You're in control now. You're in charge of your choosing. Arlene, can you imagine what it would be like to be in charge of your own choosing in the situations you described with men?

ARLENE: Yes, I've got a vivid imagination.

COUNSELLOR: Now, I would like you to do that. But I don't want you to do that unless you choose to do it your way. So you choose how you are going to imagine changing in those situations. Maybe it will be a little at a time, or all at once, or some specific thing you choose to change ... just go at the pace you need to go at ...

ARLENE: Mmm ... right ... well, I am sitting in a restaurant and I see myself being confident and not expecting too much ... my voice is ... rich like the creamy soup I am drinking and I am thinking ... how easy it is to choose to enjoy my food and the man I am with. He has an interesting view of life. It's different from mine and as the evening goes on ... I start to feel quite comfortable with myself. I can see how by choosing kind thoughts I am feeling better ... I leave some of the dessert and I enjoy the strong earthy flavour of the roasted coffee ... (Counsellor is silent for 10 minutes as Arlene talks herself through new choices and feeds it back to the counsellor.)

COUNSELLOR: Thanks, Arlene, that was great. You can continue to enjoy your choosing and changing the way you feel as long as you need to ...

Analysis

We can see how these case examples illustrate unhelpful and helpful challenging. Case One is full of unhelpful challenging. The counsellor takes challenging to mean adopting a combative attitude towards the client. So Lloyd is exposed to the counsellor's views of right and wrong and insensitive criticism. Challenging, for the counsellor in Case Two, is quite different. The counsellor adopts the attitude that challenging is a more subtle process, a process whereby the counsellor progressively enables clients to re-examine their thoughts, feelings and behaviours and the way they are attempting to satisfy their needs. Challenging is viewed as making it possible for clients to consider new directions and choices in the way they are trying to satisfy their personal needs. Lloyd faced a counsellor who played the expert and assumed what the client was thinking and feeling without checking it. Also the counsellor dwelt on Lloyd's past 'failings' and offered solutions that were inappropriate. The counsellor also seemed to set the pace which suited him and ignored the way in which Lloyd might approach choosing and changing himself, his feelings, thoughts, his behaviour or the situation he was experiencing.

Conversely, Arlene had a counsellor who engaged in helpful challenging, made it possible for Arlene to review her situation and how she felt about it, and to move towards expressing the need to get more control over her life. Clearly, the counsellor worked with Arlene and facilitated the way she could look at her choosing and imagine the kinds of changes she would like to make to regain the control she said she wanted. The counsellor did a lot of congratulating with Arlene and helped her to recreate the feelings of being 'relaxed and settled'. Arlene was also reminded of choices that were in her control. All of these things were part of the subtle process of challenging the client.

This analysis has deliberately left out some of the other unhelpful and helpful verbal challenging skills used by the counsellors. What do you think they might have been? How would these make a difference to the counselling sessions?

Which specific *non-verbal* skills do you think or feel could lead to unhelpful challenging? Why? Which specific *non-verbal* skills do you think or feel are likely to result in helpful challenging? Why?

Practice

●

Get together with a friend or colleague and carry out this exercise in pairs. Take turns to play the role of counsellor and the client. The client should talk about anything that is of current concern to them. For the first five minutes the counsellor should deliberately engage in unhelpful challenging with the client. After five minutes the counsellor switches to helpful challenging.

After you have played both roles and engaged in unhelpful and helpful challenging share and compare the experiences with each other. Include in your discussions what you thought and felt about the different kinds of challenging and how this affected any choices you needed to make in your life.

An extension of this exercise is to test how helpful your challenging skills are with your clients. However, this should be approached carefully. Provided you feel quite secure with your clients and have appropriate supervision, you can ask your clients for feedback about what was most helpful or unhelpful for them in their counselling sessions. Handled carefully and sensitively, this can be useful for the client, and it is also another way in which you can test how well your skills are transferring into practical counselling.

If this is too threatening, your supervisor or colleague can sit in on a counselling session if you have the permission of your client, and give you feedback later on the efficacy of your challenging skills and the way these hindered or helped your client to deal with the choices being faced.

Review

●

Clients come to counselling because the choices they are making are not satisfying their personal needs. Sometimes these choices are ones which clients are aware of; others are outside their awareness at present. The conscious choices they make may satisfy or frustrate their needs and have adaptive or maladaptive consequences for them. They may also think, feel, say and do many things which are preconscious and these are often associated with the habits they have developed over weeks, months or even years. The counsellors' task in practical counselling is to enable clients to uncover and become fully aware of the choices they are making and how these inhibit or facilitate changes they wish to make in themselves or their situation. Personal change may not always come about through helping clients appreciate the choices they are making that prevent them from changing. However, counsellors create the opportunity for change with their clients, by uncovering and challenging their choices. Challenging the choosing of clients can be unhelpful or helpful to the client.

Unhelpful challenging blocks progress in counselling. It also runs a high risk of breaking rapport. Unhelpful challenging can be damaging to clients and make it difficult for them to feel secure enough to risk making and experiencing the changes that different choices could have on their lives. At worst, unhelpful challenging can entrench clients in their current pattern of choosing.

Conversely, helpful challenging of the choices clients are making in their lives makes it possible for clients to re-examine, re-experience, reconsider, recognize and reorganize the choices they can act on in the future. Counsellors have the dual responsibility to ensure they avoid the worst pitfalls of unhelpful challenging and to develop and continue to maintain an appropriate level of competence in helpful challenging skills.

I always feel like there is a solution
NOLAN BUSHNELL
Don't accept that, just because a thing has been done a
certain way, it will always have to be that way
MARK MCCORMACK

Chapter 12

TASK FLEXIBILITY & PERSONAL OUTCOMES

Preparation

•

To change, clients must want to change. In practical counselling this means working with clients on choosing the personal outcomes they wish to experience, the tasks before them that will enable them to reach this experience, and the degree of flexibility they can adopt in pursuing the tasks that lead to the experiences they say they need.

Personal Outcomes

•

Counselling has come a long way when you have reached this point with your clients. Now it becomes important to find out with clients what kinds of personal outcomes they want to accomplish in their efforts to satisfy their needs. Counselling for personal outcomes involves more than simple goal setting with clients. Personal outcomes are goal-oriented. However, they are concerned with internal as well as external specific and general changes. In addition they are highly individual. Personal outcomes are personal. In this respect, practical counselling is aimed at establishing with clients the personal outcomes they want to experience in their lives. Another way of understanding this is for the counsellor to realize that clients need to think, know and feel committed to the goals they wish to accomplish.

Tackling Tasks
●

This is not always an easy job. A new struggle can emerge for clients and counsellors at this stage in the counselling process. It is discovering the tasks that clients can pursue in their attempts to realize the personal outcomes they have set for themselves. The counsellor's contribution to the tasks to be tackled by the client is one for each counsellor to work out with each client. I find this does vary greatly. Some clients prefer to take charge of this part of the counselling process. If the earlier counselling sessions have gone well, your clients will have become used to assuming some responsibility for their own decisions, feelings, thoughts, choices and actions. In these instances, they will readily proceed and carry out the tasks intended to lead to their personal outcomes. However, some clients may need tasks set for them by the counsellor in a more direct manner. In either case, the counsellor should be vigilant and adopt the attitude of 'giving the clients what they need'. The general principle here is for the counsellor to empower the client to find the energy, commitment and resolution to engage in the tasks chosen, selected and agreed in the counselling session. How the tasks are given, and what these are, depends on the particular dynamics between each counsellor and client at any particular time.

One other thing about tasks. These are usually engaged in by the client outside the counselling session. Tasks are things clients often take away with them to work on *between* counselling sessions. So, for example, let's say one of the tasks that a client has been set, or has suggested himself, is 'to remain silent and listen to his partner instead of arguing with her'. And let's also say that the personal outcome desired was a reduction in arguments at home. The client then has the job of carrying out this task and bringing back the results of his experiences to you in the next counselling session. Typically, in the session, the client can be congratulated on his effort and the experience of conducting this task can then be explored with the client. Other tasks can be engaged in by clients *during* counselling sessions. For instance, clients can also adopt the task of summarizing and feeding back how they are experiencing the counselling session or reviewing what they have learned during a counselling session. Another example might be a client who regularly has a short relaxation session before talking with her counsellor. Here the client could easily set up her own relaxation session during counselling. She could play the relaxation tape and get into a more relaxed state, and then go on to the next stage of the counselling session.

Clients in crisis may need to be more directed in the tasks they need to tackle — at least in the short term. For example, faced with a client who reveals that he has a compulsive gambling problem and has run up devastating debts, the counsellor may have to arrange with him for the surrender of his credit cards and a specific credit management plan. All this would be necessary in the short term, whilst at the same time the counsellor could begin to explore the alternative ways in which the client could better manage his compulsion to gamble, or the effects gambling is having on his personal life. Clearly, counsellors need to make careful judgements about how directive they are with clients in the tasks pursued in counselling. In order to do this well, they need to be flexible in their approach to counselling clients. Flexibility on the part of the counsellor in practical counselling does one other thing that is essential to good practice. It provides clients with a role model that encourages them to be more flexible in the choices they make, and the tasks they adopt.

Flexibility

●

Flexibility frees clients to experiment with pursuing tasks and experiencing their personal outcomes. People often end up in counselling simply because they have not been flexible enough in the way they are trying to satisfy their personal needs. These clients seem to have either a very narrow repertoire of ways to run their lives or are too rigid in their thinking and feelings and beliefs about what should be done to solve their problems. It is often not for the want of trying to solve their problems. You can probably recall clients saying to you, "God knows how I have tried." Indeed, it may be in the very trying that some clients worsen, maintain and perpetuate the very problems they wish to overcome. Some counsellors have gone so far as to say that clients have problems because they try to solve them. In my view, it is not so much the trying but the lack of flexibility clients have in the way they try to solve their difficulties that maintains and perpetuates, or even increases, their personal misery.

I am reminded of a teacher who came to counselling because he had turned up at work drunk and the children in his class had noticed it, and so did his colleagues on the teaching staff. After a warning it happened again. This time he was disciplined and asked if he could see a counsellor. It turned out he needed to feel included in what was going on in the school but he felt too inhibited and underconfident to 'join in'. His solution was to "drink just enough scotch to let myself go". His outcome was clear. However, the way he went about trying to satisfy his need to be involved with other people wasn't sufficiently flexible. He eventually became dependent on alcohol, relying on it more and more to satisfy his need to be with other people. Unfortunately, he seemed unprepared, or not ready, to try another way of losing his inhibitions and building up his confidence. The result was that he lost his job and his marriage broke up.

Not everyone who comes to counselling solves their problems. Not everyone is ready to be more flexible and try different ways of satisfying their needs and overcoming the frustrations and disappointments they experience in life. However, against this fact is the counter-fact that many clients who come to counselling realize sooner or later that they want to be, and can be, more flexible in the ways they think, feel and act.

Every client has a potential for change. But not every client will change. Yet it is this potential for client change that the counsellor works with throughout the whole process of practical counselling. Building rapport, listening, discovering relevant information, making choices, knowing what outcomes clients wish to experience and the tasks they need to pursue to satisfy their needs are the main skills that counsellors bring to bear on the counselling process. Working together in this way counsellors can empower clients to find new solutions to old problems, old solutions to new problems, and new solutions for new problems. Counselling sessions provide the context within which clients can become strong enough to identify the outcomes they wish to experience in their lives, the tasks that lie before them, and the degree of flexibility they have in finding new ways of satisfying their personal needs.

The Mountain Metaphor

●

You may find it useful to think of personal outcomes, tasks and flexibility like two climbers faced with a mountain. The ascent of the mountain represents the personal problems or difficulties the client and the counsellor face during counselling. The two climbers are the counsellor and the client.

The peaks of the mountain are the personal outcomes of the client. The counsellor and client face climbing the mountain together. Now, the mountain may be large or small. And it can be very near or some way off in the distance. It may have one single peak or many peaks, and these peaks can be large or small. Some of the peaks seem easy to scale and others more difficult; some are smooth and safe and others jagged and dangerous.

The two climbers need to be prepared to choose which peaks they want to scale and how they are going to go about the task of their climb. They may decide to take it in turns to help each other up the specific peaks. Sometimes one of the climbers will be more experienced and skilful and lead the other climber on parts of their journey. But the climbers work with each other, each giving of their skills to climb the mountain. Now the way they climb the mountain can turn out very interesting. If it is familiar territory, the climbers may make rapid progress and celebrate their achievement and congratulate each other for helping each other along the way. On unsure ground, they may take more time to make progress and need to trust each other's skill even more, so that they can support each other in climbing a new peak for the first time. They need to be prepared to deal with setbacks that can occur along the way. If they look back too often, or ignore the risks, they may give up the climb or, worse still, fall off the mountain.

In climbing the mountain, the climbers may rely on tried and proven routes to get to where they are going, and this may work. However, there will be times when the easier route to the top of the mountain may be blocked. Then our intrepid climbers can do one of three things. They can try to continue along the same route in the same way. This is likely to prove to be time-consuming and exhausting for the climbers and show little result for their efforts. Another thing they can do is to go back to the safety of their base camp to work out what to do next. Although this may take time, it is likely to be a temporary retreat. Finally, they can find a new way of overcoming the obstruction, maybe a way they had never thought of climbing before, and, perhaps feeling differently about this new way of getting to the top of the mountain, the climbers can then continue with their climb. Some climbers will reach the top of the mountain. Some will attain a lesser peak. But they all will have earned the appropriate recognition they so rightly deserve for their climb.

Exercise

● In what respects are counsellors and clients engaged in practical counselling similar to our climbers? How are they different?
● What have you learned personally as a counsellor from the mountain metaphor?
● How could you use the mountain metaphor with clients in practical counselling?
● In which specific additional ways could counsellors benefit from a deeper understanding of the mountain metaphor in practical counselling?

Case Examples

1 • Vera

VERA: I don't know what to do now. I've tried everything to lose weight.

COUNSELLOR: Everything?

VERA: Well, you know, I know what I want.

COUNSELLOR: Yes?

VERA: To look good.

COUNSELLOR: Look good?

VERA: Diets don't work. Group dieting is just an excuse for me to go and binge again.

COUNSELLOR: Your task is simple, Vera. Get down to the right weight for your height, keep at it for six weeks and never eat in-between meals. Keep away from chocolate and chips, and come and see me in six weeks.

VERA: I don't think that will work. I've tried it before.

COUNSELLOR: Try harder and you will get results. Now make an appointment to see me in six weeks' time . . . thanks for coming.

VERA: Right, I'm sure it is going to be as bad when I see you again.

COUNSELLOR: We'll see.

VERA *(Gets up and leaves counselling room shaking her head)*:

2 • Simon

SIMON: My confidence is rock bottom and I will never get it back this time. *(Sighs and wipes some tears from his eyes)*

COUNSELLOR *(Sighs and blinks his eyes as he replies to Simon)*:
It sounds as if you're really feeling bad. You believe there is no way back at the moment.

SIMON: Yes ... I have tried ... drink, drugs, and I am worried about them as well, I think it's the only way. I lose either way, I am worried ...

COUNSELLOR: So worried you might go back to them and that might be another problem you can feel bad about?

SIMON: No, I am only concerned about losing my confidence.

COUNSELLOR: And drink and drugs give you confidence.

SIMON: Yeh, at least the illusion of being confident. I really want to be more confident in myself.

COUNSELLOR: If you take away the illusion and you are really more confident in yourself, how does that look, and how do you feel now, Simon? Just run those thoughts and feelings through in your mind for a few moments ... now ...

SIMON *(becomes more animated and his mood lightens)*:   Oh, that's easy, I would stand differently, I would speak without worrying about what I had to say, and I would be able to initiate contact with people instead of waiting for them to talk to me. I wouldn't even think about being shy, I would feel great. *(Colour comes into Simon's cheeks and he smiles.)*

COUNSELLOR: Like you're feeling now?

SIMON *(sounding surprised)*:   Yes, Yes.

COUNSELLOR: That's great. How did you do that, Simon?

SIMON: Do what?

COUNSELLOR: That great feeling you just experienced.

SIMON: I thought how I really would be when I am confident and the great feeling just came.

COUNSELLOR: Isn't it interesting how you can produce that great feeling by just thinking about it? Simon, you can manage to do things differently.

SIMON: Yes, I'm honestly confused, amazed really.

COUNSELLOR: I mean, you never slipped in any drugs or had a quick half bottle of scotch when you were doing it, did you? And you experienced this feeling, it's great!

SIMON *(briefly laughs and smiles broadly)*: No, but I would like to keep on having that good feeling just by thinking about it. I want that feeling more often . . . more and more. It is great.

COUNSELLOR: Great, Simon, you know this feeling and by thinking about it in this way you can have this feeling more often. You know this great feeling and it's your thinking that gives you this great feeling. Let's find out how you can use this new way of experiencing your great feeling more and more...

Analysis

The counsellor in Case One starts off very well. Using reflecting back and some of the structure of the client's language the counsellor develops some rapport. However, this is quickly lost, and the counsellor then proceeds to fall into the trap of advising the client. How did this happen?

First of all, the counsellor leaps forward into choosing and providing the task for the client. Also the counsellor does not check with Vera if the task is one which is appropriate or if she is motivated to carry it out. Clearly, even a cursory glance at Vera's replies or her non-verbal signals suggest she is unlikely or unwilling to carry out the tasks set by the counsellor.

The counsellor was not flexible enough to work with Vera or discover the personal outcomes Vera wanted for herself. No attempt was made by the counsellor to enable Vera to discover what needs she was trying to satisfy. Indeed, instead of creating the conditions in counselling where Vera could consider alternative ways of satisfying her personal needs, the counsellor blocks this off. This is all achieved by the counsellor. It is done by advice giving, lack of flexibility, ignoring the personal outcomes of the client, and pursuing a task that is of interest to the counsellor but not the client.

Now let's examine Case Two. It is quite different. In Case Two, the counsellor develops rapid rapport with Simon. This is maintained throughout the session. The counsellor strengthens the rapport and uses the structure of Simon's language to begin the search for finding a new way of experiencing his problems. To do this Simon is asked to imagine what it would be like and how it would feel if he were confident. The counsellor tests an 'as if you were confident' approach with Simon, on a hunch that Simon can produce good feelings by thinking about a good experience. This hunch pays off. Simon re-experiences a 'great feeling' and allows himself to enjoy the experience. The counsellor makes a point of asking Simon how he managed to bring the good feelings about. Simon reaches his own conclusion and tells the counsellor he did it by thinking about how he would like to be. He also tells the counsellor he wants more of the good feelings he experienced. This is in clear contrast to the counsellor who told Vera what she should do to lose weight.

The lessons from these cases show how important it is to create and maintain rapport with our clients. They also illustrate how the counsellor can use a similar language structure and content to the client. Along with this, we see how flexibility on the part of the counsellor makes it possible to test with clients new ways in which they can achieve their personal outcomes and satisfy their needs. Showing clients how they can discover what tasks lie before them and how they can experience the outcomes they wish to accomplish is all part of counsellor flexibility. The counsellor in Case One was inflexible, gave advice, presumed the outcome for Vera and prescribed the task she should undertake. In Case Two, the counsellor worked with Simon's wishes, his decisions, the tasks before him, what he wanted and how he managed to bring his desired outcome about. Which approach do you prefer? Why?

Practice

●

Session One

Pair up with a colleague or friend, or someone you know who is willing to volunteer as a 'client' and experience what it is like working with a counsellor who is inflexible, gives advice and pre- scribes the outcomes clients should have and how they ought to bring them about. You play the part of the counsellor. Set aside 15 minutes and carry out a counselling session with your 'client' using this approach.

When you have completed the session, review the experience for the client and the counsellor. What was it like? How would you change the way the session went, and what, if anything, would you keep the same? Write down your conclusions or record your session on audio- or video-tape.

Break for 5–10 minutes.

Session Two

Now pair up again for another 15 minute session.

This time, adopt the skills involved in building and maintaining rapport, gathering information and working with the client's choices about satisfying personal needs. Link these together through your counsellor flexibility and utilize them to empower your clients to discover their personal outcomes and the tasks they can engage in to experience and satisfy their needs.

Once again, on completion of the session, review your experi- ences as client and counsellor. What was different this time? What seemed the same? Where were you most satisfied with the session as counsellor/as client? Which specific skills or attitudes were the most significant in the session? Why?

Remember to keep a record of what you have learned by writ- ing your conclusions down or recording the session on audio- or video-tape.

Review

●

Clients usually come to counselling because they have personal problems. They want to change something in themselves or in their lives. Many clients succeed in making changes that are important to them and this is facilitated through their counselling sessions. However, not all clients manage to accomplish these changes. Sometimes the explanation is simply that the clients are not ready to make significant changes in themselves or their lives. At other times they may be ready to change but not know what it is they need to change to live a more satisfying life. There are also those occasions when counsellors may inadvertently make it difficult for their clients to change. Some clients may require more directing by the counsellor, especially in times of crisis. It follows therefore that the counsellor may find that there are times when it is entirely appropriate to be directive with a client and at others the counsellor looks to the client for the direction the counselling session will take.

In practical counselling the effective counsellor adopts a flexible attitude towards helping clients discover what it is they want to change and how they will bring change about in their lives. To do this the effective counsellor enables clients to work with the personal outcomes they want to experience and the tasks that need to be undertaken to better manage or overcome their problems.

The essential principle is not for the counsellor to be directive or non-directive. It is to be flexible. The ineffective counsellor is one who is rigid and wishes to achieve his or her own outcomes, even at the expense of clients. The effective counsellor is one who is flexible in enabling clients to recognize their needs, choose the outcomes they wish to experience, and the tasks they can adopt towards living a more satisfying life.

Chapter 13

PRACTICAL COUNSELLING SKILLS IN PERSPECTIVE

Using Your Counselling Skills

•

Congratulations! You are now ready to start putting your practical counselling skills to work. You can now take your counselling skills and use them with your colleagues and clients. The emphasis is on *using* your practical counselling skills. Practice makes perfect. If you don't practise your counselling skills, then you run a high risk of becoming deskilled. Regular practice also helps you to integrate the skills you are learning. When our practical counselling skills are integrated with each other we raise our level of personal competence as counsellors. Personal competence is the goal every counsellor aspires to. It enables us to provide the best possible counselling we can to our clients.

Personal Responsibility and Counsellor Supervision

•

How this is done depends on counsellors taking personal responsibility for maintaining their own well-being, general health and competence to practise counselling. You have probably acquired a number of the counselling skills outlined in this book and perhaps you have already started using your new-found counselling skills with your clients. For those people who are already experienced counsellors, you may have had the opportunity of using some additional counselling skills as well as consolidating those skills in which you are already competent to practise.

Whether you are just starting off in practical counselling or are already an experienced counsellor, it is likely you have realized the desirability or necessity of arranging supervision. Supervision is part of practical counselling. It is something that all responsible people using practical counselling skills can have available to them. It is not mandatory to make arrangements to have supervision. The choice is yours. However, there are many compelling reasons why counsellors should seriously consider seeking supervision with an appropriately qualified person. Here are some of the most important ones.

Seeking appropriate counsellor supervision:

1 Provides counsellors with a nurturing relationship in which they can find personal support and encouragement;
2 Facilitates the professional development of counsellors;
3 Creates a climate where counsellors can ensure they are practising counselling responsibly with their clients;
4 Enables counsellors to maintain their standards of personal competence with their clients;
5 Opens up opportunities for counsellors to avoid or manage personal crisis;
6 Provides a context for considering problems connected with client confidentiality;
7 Makes it possible to discuss and examine ethical issues pertinent to the practice of counselling;
8 Offers a place where client–counsellor role relationships and boundaries can be assessed, reviewed and clarified;
9 Presents counsellors with an opportunity for their continuing personal and professional development;
10 Constructs a framework where counsellors can deal with personal stress arising out of their work with clients.

The Counsellor and the Supervision Climate

Appropriate supervision can provide a social climate where counsellors are enabled to express, explore and understand their own concerns in relationship to the work they do with clients. In many ways supervision, when conducted well, is like a mirror image of the client–counsellor relationship. Confidentiality is established within the boundaries of the supervisory relationship. The counsellor feels valued by the supervisor. Rapport and trust are present. Information is shared and compared. Perceptions and choices for the counsellor are reviewed. Counsellors also consider changes they may wish to make in themselves or the way they provide counselling to clients. At other times, counsellors can work through their thoughts, feelings and the actions they might take with specific clients.

We could say the supervisor has a responsibility to create a facilitative social climate in counsellor supervision. Just as the counsellor has the responsibility of creating the conditions for change with the client, so too the supervisor has the obligation of creating appropriate conditions for supervision with the counsellor. However, it is important to realize and accept that it is the counsellor who is finally responsible for any decisions he or she makes as a result of supervision sessions. Counsellors therefore must also be careful not to allow undue supervisory pressures to interfere with their methods of counselling or their decisions with clients in counselling.

The Competence Learning Cycle in Counselling

●

Another essential is for counsellors to be competent in using practical counselling skills with their clients. Counsellor supervision should ensure that appropriate counselling skills are maintained. Counsellors should not allow themselves to get 'rusty'. If the counsellor becomes deskilled it can only be unhelpful to clients and may, in some cases, even be damaging to their well-being. This is a top priority for those people who already practise counselling with clients. If you are in this group, the message is stark but clear: stay competent.

For those people who are aspiring counsellors, or carers who are new to counselling and wish to use practical counselling skills, there is also a simple but vital rule: become competent. Don't just hope you will become good at using practical counselling skills. Above all, please do not think all you have to do is to like people to become effective in counselling clients. Liking people may help, but it is not enough. Serious students and practitioners of counselling need to be skilful in what they do. They are open to learning the skills of practical counselling. They are motivated. They believe in what they are doing.

Acquiring practical counselling skills is a bit like learning to ride a bicycle. Do you remember how you learned to ride one? When I have asked people on counselling skills courses this question, they come up with answers like "I didn't know how at first", "I got tangled up in the pedals", "I was so busy pointing it in the right direction I forgot how to use the brakes." Others have said, "I knew what I was supposed to do but I just fell off, I couldn't keep my balance", "I was so busy concentrating on doing what I was told I forgot", "Once I got the hang of it, I was off", and "I didn't realize it, suddenly I could do it and I never thought about it — I was on my own and was cycling."

These reflections on what it was like to learn to ride a bicycle give us a useful guideline about the competence learning cycle that takes place in acquiring practical counselling skills. This can be readily appreciated when we map out the competence learning cycle and consider how it applies to the acquisition, practice and maintenance of counselling skills.

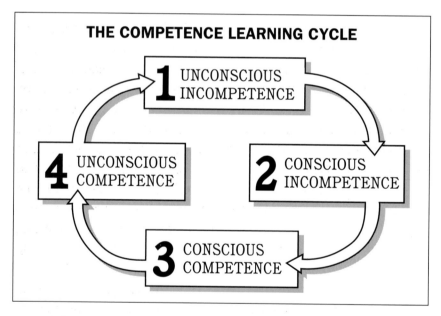

THE COMPETENCE LEARNING CYCLE

1 UNCONSCIOUS INCOMPETENCE

2 CONSCIOUS INCOMPETENCE

3 CONSCIOUS COMPETENCE

4 UNCONSCIOUS COMPETENCE

Imagine, for a moment, that we are new to counselling and we want to become competent in using practical counselling skills. With the competence learning cycle we can see that at first we may be largely unconscious of our incompetence to practise counselling skills. However, after some self-awareness training or education, this can soon give way to becoming conscious of our incompetence and restricted range of counselling skills. Following this, we can then embark on the conscious application of practical counselling skills. During this period of learning we can become conscious of our 'errors' as well as using our new-found counselling skills. We now know what practical counselling skills are, and when we are using them. Conversely, we know what they are not and sometimes find ourselves falling into 'old habits' such as giving advice and telling clients what they should do to better their lives. We become conscious of some incompetence in our practical counselling skills and move towards becoming consciously competent. As we practise, though, there comes a moment when we are less aware of trying to provide practical counselling. What seems to happen is that we become unconsciously competent. We can integrate our counselling skills so that they seem natural and 'seamless' in our work with clients. When this happens we do not labour in an effort to use practical counselling skills with our clients. We can, however, reflect on the skills that were used in any particular counselling session at its conclusion.

The learning competence cycle can be used in many innovative ways. I have found three ways that I would like to share with you. The first way the learning competence cycle can be used is for practising counsellors to reflect on their current level of practical counselling skills. Doing this often helps counsellors to engage in some self-counselling and reach decisions about future skills development for themselves. A second way the cycle can be used is on counselling skills courses and training events. I find those who are fairly new to counselling are enlightened and encouraged. It is particularly evident when they experience moving away from the unconscious incompetence end of the learning cycle towards conscious competence in practical counselling skills.

Third, and related to the other uses of the competence learning cycle, is the part it can play in supervision sessions. The supervisor and counsellor can find a common starting point for their supervision session using the competence learning cycle. Sometimes this will mean exploring new skills or strengthening existing ones, or it can be used as a basis for providing helpful feedback. The competence learning cycle also helps to focus the supervision session. In this sense it is of great value to the counsellor, the student of counselling skills, and supervisors.

It is important to remember that the competence learning cycle is conceptualized as a cycle. Becoming competent in practical counselling skills is a desirable goal. However, staying competent is crucial if clients are to benefit from their counselling sessions. Therefore it follows that we shall all — from time to time — need to return to the competence cycle. As well as maintaining the essential practical counselling skills, there will be new skills to learn and new competences to acquire.

Clearly, I believe the competence learning cycle is a more than useful guide for counsellors and all wishing to continue to use practical counselling skills in their work with clients.

Counselling for Counsellors
●

Appropriate supervision and competence to practise make it more likely that we will be effective in using counselling skills with clients. However, all of this could count for nothing if we do not also provide counselling for counsellors. Counselling can be stressful and demanding for counsellors. In the writings, research, training and counselling workshops that I have conducted over the past 10 years, I have found a consistently emerging theme. Counselling clients can be personally very taxing on counsellors. High levels of stress and burnout are not uncommon in those who provide counselling. There are counsellors who have difficulty in coping with caring. These counsellors can become so burdened with their clients' problems that they become the victims of counselling. They are the wounded healers. Sometimes I have become so moved by the plight of counsellors, I have likened counselling clients to the dangers of smoking. I have even gone so far as to suggest that those who provide counselling to clients should have imprinted signs in their minds that read 'Counselling can damage your health'!

We have seen how, in practical counselling, it is essential for counsellors to adopt and express a caring attitude towards their clients. However, some counsellors can care overmuch for their clients. I know this because I see some of these counsellors in my own clinics for counsellors. Who are these counsellors? They are counsellors who are always available to their clients. They are counsellors who have no clear boundaries between their personal lives and the counselling they make available to clients. They are counsellors who override and overlook their own needs. They are counsellors who care too much. They are, potentially, you and me.

Now, I am going to say something that may shock and surprise you. If you are seriously interested in practical counselling, don't care overmuch for your clients.

Overcaring can damage your personal health and well-being. Curiously, overcaring can have adverse consequences for clients as well as counsellors. This is one of the paradoxes of practical counselling. When overcaring leads to stress and burnout in counsellors, a number of undesirable outcomes can occur. Such counsellors can become deskilled, demotivated, depressed and uninterested in their clients. Some may even think, feel and behave as if they dislike or resent their clients.

Clearly, we should aim to avoid stress and burnout. It is counter-productive for clients and counsellors. Overcaring needs to be kept in check and a balanced perspective of positive regard for clients maintained. This way, counsellors can remain compe-tent to use the counselling skills they have developed for the intended benefit of their clients.

Counselling counsellors can act as a safeguard for both coun-sellors and their clients. It may not ensure competence in coun-selling clients. But what it can do is alleviate counsellor stress and burnout and reduce the probability of damage to clients as a result of incompetent counselling. Making counselling available for counsellors is one way we can avoid the ravages of overcaring in the provision of counselling to clients. How this is done is up to individual counsellors and their employing organizations. Fortunately, support and counselling are now more readily avail-able for staff providing counselling services to clients. Counsellor supervision, competence to practise and counselling for counsel-lors all help to put practical counselling in perspective. Practical counselling is for clients. However, it is also for the vast army of providers of counselling. A perspective on practical counselling which ignores the needs either of counsellors or of clients lacks depth and understanding of the counselling process. Employed for any length of time, it can only lead to troubled counsellors and troubled counsellor–client relationships.

Practice

●

Meet other counsellors, supervisors or colleagues and explore the arguments for and against counsellor supervision. What view or position do you take? Why? If you are persuaded of the need for counsellor supervision what arrangements for supervision should you make?

Get together with a colleague or your work group or another counsellor and share and compare all of your present range of practical counselling skills with each other. Now set up some practice sessions using your colleague, group or counsellor. Use as many of your practical counselling skills as seem appropriate to the practice sessions.

When you have completed these sessions congratulate each other on the skills you have used. Now give and receive feedback on the skills you feel competent in and those you need to develop further.

Keep records of sessions, either on audio-tape or written, for your own use in the future.

How important is it to provide counselling for counsellors? What can happen if counselling for counsellors is not provided? What specific counselling for counsellors is available to you? How far has your organization explicitly acknowledged the need for support and counselling for counsellors? Outline the plans or services your organization has for counselling counsellors.

Practical Counselling Skills
An Overview

●

Practical counselling skills get us started in counselling. They do not make us expert counsellors. However, we have begun to understand more about counselling and how it can be practised with clients. Those who are already counsellors will have had the opportunity of strengthening skills they are already familiar with and acquiring some new practical skills to add to their existing personal competence as counsellors. Whatever our level of counselling ability, we have seen how our practical counselling skills need to be developed and maintained to a high degree of competence. It is for this reason that practical counselling has something valuable to offer carers new to counselling as well as those more experienced in this field of helping.

We have taken the view that practical counselling is about influencing clients in a special way. Practical counselling is about empowering clients to make changes and choices in their lives. Those carers who provide practical counselling can make it more possible for clients to satisfy their personal needs. The influencing that goes on in practical counselling is aimed at utilizing the as yet untapped personal resources of clients. Clients solve their own problems. It is through the judicious application of practical counselling skills that counsellors enable their clients to discover abilities they have not used for some time or to develop new ways of satisfying their needs and overcoming their personal problems.

In practical counselling, there are counsellor tasks and client tasks. Discovering what these tasks are and how they can be accomplished constitutes the heart of practical counselling.

Working with practical counselling skills, the counsellor and the client embark on a journey together. This journey is facilitated through the building of rapport with the client, uncovering relevant information, and working with client choices to make changes aimed at satisfying their needs. The more flexible counsellors and clients can be in utilizing their combined resources for this purpose, the more likely that clients can make desirable changes in the way they think, feel and behave within themselves, towards others and in the situations that concern them. These changes may be small and specific or larger and affect many areas of the client's life.

Practical counselling is founded on a working alliance between the client and the counsellor. The stronger this working alliance is, the greater the opportunity for clients to live a more satisfying life. However, there will be times when this alliance breaks down. Sometimes this will be through no fault of the counsellor. Sometimes it may be deliberately precipitated by the counsellor. And on other occasions it will be tested by the client.

Now and then counsellors may jeopardize the working alliance between themselves and their clients through ignorance or lack of competence in their counselling skills. In an ideal world this should never happen. In practice it can and does. It is a risk all counsellors take when they see a client. As counsellors new to, or familiar with, practical counselling, we have an overriding responsibility to minimize this risk to our clients and ourselves.

There are three useful safeguards we can responsibly and seriously consider if we are to avoid risking harm to our clients or ourselves as a result of counselling sessions. First, we can consider arranging regular and appropriate counsellor supervision for ourselves. Second, we can seriously consider how we can remain competent in a wide range of practical counselling skills, and how and when new skills can be developed and maintained in our work with clients. Third, we can consider how counselling for counsellors can be best made available to us and prevent, or at the very least limit, the ravages of counsellor stress and burnout. When we have sufficiently considered these safeguards for ourselves and our clients, we need to choose and act. We can choose and act on some, all or none of these safeguards that are open to us. Whatever we do, we should be guided by a principle pertinent to all practical counselling. Our choices and actions as counsellors should always be guided by how best we can provide responsible and competent counselling to our clients.

BIBLIOGRAPHY

Bailey R, *Coping with Stress in Caring*, Blackwell Scientific, Oxford, 1986.

Bailey R, *50 Activities for Managing Stress*, Gower, Aldershot, 1989.

Bailey R, *50 Activities for Developing Counselling Skills*, Gower, Aldershot, 1991.

Bailey R & Clarke M, *Stress and Coping in Nursing*, Chapman and Hall, London, 1990.

Cameron–Bandler L, *Solutions Future*, Pace Books, San Rafael, California, 1985.

Edelwich J & K Brodsky A, 'Burn-out: Stages of Disillusionment' in *The Helping Professions*, The Human Sciences Press, New York, 1980.

Egan G, *The Skilled Helper*, Brookes/Cole, Indiana, California, 1986.

Eisenberg S & Delaney D, *The Counselling Process*, Rand McNally, Chicago, 1977.

Erickson M, *A Teaching Seminar with Milton H Erickson* (ed. Zeig JK), Brunner–Mezel, New York, 1980.

Glasser R, *Reality Therapy*, Harper & Row, London, 1975.

Glasser R, *Control Theory*, Harper & Row, London, 1985.

Hobson R, *Forms of Feeling*, Tavistock Publications, London, 1985.

Jourard SM, *The Transparent Self*, Van Norstrand, New Jersey, 1964.

Lankton S, *Practical Magic*, Meta Publications, Cupertino, California, 1980.

Lazarus R, 'The Stress and Coping Paradigm' in *Theoretical Bases for Psychopathology* (eds. Eidorfer C, Cohen D, Kleinman A & Maxim P), Spectrum Publications, New York, 1981.

Munro E, Manthec R & Small J, *Counselling: A Skills Approach*, Methuen, London, 1979.

Nelson-Jones R, *Human Relationship Skills*, Cassell, London, 1986.

Nelson-Jones R, *The Theory and Practice of Counselling Psychology*, Cassell, London, 1991.

Rogers C, *A Way of Being*, Houghton Mifflin, Boston, 1980.

Rogers C, *On Becoming A Person*, Constable, London, 1986.

Schutz W, *Joy*, Harper & Row, New York, 1967.

Schutz W, *Profound Simplicity*, Turnstone Books, London, 1979.

Client and staff services

For further details of client services, staff training courses, and seminars and workshops in counselling, cognitive psychotherapy, neurolinguistic programming, hypnotherapy and other psychological therapies please contact:

Roy Bailey PhD CPsychol AFBPsS
c/o Winslow Press
Telford Road
Bicester
Oxon
OX6 0TS
United Kingdom